MOUNTAINS
of the
YORKSHIRE DALES

Hillside Guides - Across the North

Yorkshire Photobook • JOURNEY OF THE WHARFE

Hillwalking • MOUNTAINS OF THE YORKSHIRE DALES

Easy Walks • 50 YORKSHIRE WALKS FOR ALL

Short Scenic Walks (30 Walks)
- THREE PEAKS & MALHAM
- WHARFEDALE & ILKLEY
- SOUTH PENNINES
- RIBBLE VALLEY & BOWLAND
- ARNSIDE & LUNESDALE
- NORTH YORK MOORS
- WENSLEYDALE
- HARROGATE & NIDDERDALE
- HAWORTH & AIRE VALLEY
- PENDLE & LANCASHIRE MOORS
- AMBLESIDE & SOUTH LAKELAND
- TEESDALE & WEARDALE

Short Scenic Walks (20 Walks)
- SEDBERGH & DENTDALE
- SWALEDALE

Walking in Yorkshire - Yorkshire Dales (25 Walks)
- East: NIDDERDALE & RIPON
- West: THREE PEAKS & HOWGILL FELLS
- South: WHARFEDALE & MALHAM
- North: WENSLEYDALE & SWALEDALE

Walking in Yorkshire - North/East (25 Walks)
- NORTH YORK MOORS South/West
- NORTH YORK MOORS North/East
- YORKSHIRE WOLDS
- HOWARDIAN HILLS & VALE OF YORK
- RICHMONDSHIRE & HAMBLETON

Walking in Yorkshire - West/South/Mid (25 Walks)
- AIRE VALLEY & BRONTE COUNTRY
- HARROGATE & ILKLEY
- CALDERDALE & SOUTH PENNINES
- SOUTH YORKSHIRE
- WEST YORKSHIRE COUNTRYSIDE

Circular Walks - Lancashire (22 Walks)
- PENDLE & the RIBBLE

Hillwalking - Lake District (25 Walks)
- LAKELAND FELLS - SOUTH
- LAKELAND FELLS - EAST
- LAKELAND FELLS - NORTH
- LAKELAND FELLS - WEST

Long Distance Walks
- COAST TO COAST WALK
- DALES WAY
- PENDLE WAY

Visit www.hillsidepublications.co.uk

MOUNTAINS of the YORKSHIRE DALES
A Hillwalker's Guide

Paul Hannon
HILLSIDE

HILLSIDE Publications
38 Westburn Avenue
Keighley
West Yorkshire
BD22 6AW

First published 2024

© Paul Hannon 2024   ISBN 978-1-907626-48-7

Cover illustrations: Pen-y-ghent; Ingleborough, Back: Buckden Pike
Page One: Pen-y-ghent Pinnacle; Page Three: Yarlside from Cautley Crag
Page 4: Widdale Fell; Page 5: Howgill Fells
(Paul Hannon/Yorkshire Photo Library)

The sketch maps are based on 1947 Ordnance Survey One-Inch maps

Printed in China on behalf of Latitude Press

> Whilst the author has walked and researched all the routes for the purposes of this guide, no responsibility can be accepted for any unforeseen circumstances encountered while following them. The publisher would appreciate information regarding material changes.

Contents

INTRODUCTION..6

WALK 1	**Great Whernside** *from Kettlewell*................10
WALK 2	**Buckden Pike** *from Buckden*.........................18
WALK 3	**Birks Fell** *from Buckden*................................24
WALK 4	**Yockenthwaite Moor** *from Hubberholme*.....28
WALK 5	**Fountains Fell** & **Darnbrook Fell** *from Rainscar*............32
WALK 6	**Pen-y-ghent** & **Plover Hill** *from Horton-in-Ribblesdale*...36
WALK 7	**Ingleborough** & **Simon Fell** *from Clapham*...................44
WALK 8	**Whernside** *from Ribblehead*........................... 54
WALK 9	**Gragareth** *from Kingsdale*..............................60
WALK 10	**Great Coum** *from Dent*....................................66
WALK 11	**Middleton Fell** *from Barbon*...........................72
WALK 12	**Widdale Fell** *from Cowgill*..............................76
WALK 13	**Dodd Fell** *from Hawes*.....................................80
WALK 14	**Wether Fell** *from Hawes*..................................84
WALK 15	**Lovely Seat** & **Great Shunner Fell** *from Thwaite*...........88
WALK 16	**Rogan's Seat** *from Keld*..................................94
WALK 17	**Nine Standards Rigg** *from Lamps Moss*.......98
WALK 18	**High Seat** *from Outhgill*.................................102
WALK 19	**Lunds Fell** *from Aisgill Moor*.........................108
WALK 20	**Swarth Fell** & **Wild Boar Fell** *from Aisgill Moor*..........114
WALK 21	**Baugh Fell** *from Garsdale Foot*......................122
WALK 22	**Yarlside** & **Randygill Top** *from Cautley*.......128
WALK 23	**Calders** & **The Calf** *from Sedbergh*.............136
WALK 24	**Fell Head** *from Carlingill*..............................144
WALK 25	**THREE PEAKS WALK** *from Horton-in-Ribblesdale*.......150

INDEX..160

Introduction

The mountains of the Yorkshire Dales are a richly varied collection of 31 breezy heights scattered around the national park. Some of these hills are nationally famous, notably the Three Peaks of Whernside, Ingleborough and Pen-y-ghent. Others are less popular but well tramped such as in Upper Wharfedale and the Howgill Fells, while some are largely unfrequented, which of course only adds to their charm: many familiar with the Dales will be unaware of the likes of Rogan's Seat and Yockenthwaite Moor. All but one are within the national park, with Nine Standards Rigg only a stone's throw distant, and itself stood within a National Landscape (previously AONB). What constitutes a separate mountain? The generally accepted requirement in England is deemed to be a 2000ft/609.6m hill needing a minimum re-ascent of 98.4ft/30m. This rightly excludes numerous minor tops that cannot realistically be claimed as separate fells.

Within these pages 24 walks take you to the summits of all 31 hills. Whilst all could be tackled individually, 7 of the routes embrace neighbouring hills whose proximity renders them logical pairings. The more ambitious could choose to merge other pairs, most notably Great Coum/Gragareth and Wether Fell/Dodd Fell, and even the Howgill Fells into one super-outing. Only one walk exceeds ten miles, and many are appreciably shorter, with the average length being around 7^1⁄$_2$ miles. Almost all walks are circular in format, with only one being a complete 'out and back' route and a couple more having only slight variations. The final route describes the classic challenge of the Three Peaks Walk, which would be difficult to omit from these pages, though the individual hills obviously feature in their own right in the book.

The book's purpose is to create a collection of practical walks, and not necessarily the easiest options. The practice of 'bagging' a summit from the nearest road-top is largely eschewed here, because surely it's about a lot more than that. Worst example would be the ascent of Lovely Seat from the Buttertubs Pass, achievable within a half-hour but surely with little sense of satisfaction. Several inconsistencies arise on the naming of fells, where writers have applied summit names to entire hills: prime example is Widdale Fell, where the summit is known as Great Knoutberry Hill, but the fell itself is without doubt Widdale Fell.

All routes are either on public rights of way or Open Access land. Some of these areas can be closed at certain times of year, notably in the nesting season from April to July, or the grouse-shooting season

Introduction

commencing on August 12th. This shouldn't infer a near-general ban, indeed most areas are open most of the time. If uncertain, seek advice at www.openaccess.naturalengland.org.uk. Dogs are banned from much Open Access land other than on public rights of way, due either to sporting interests, sheep farming or wildlife. The latter is most pertinent in springtime, when the uplands are an important habitat of declining populations of ground-nesting birds: at these times it is desirable, wherever practicable, to adhere to visibly trodden routes. The majority of walks are indeed on trodden ways, though inevitably sections on some walks have no visible path underfoot: these have been kept to a minimum. Additionally, given that these uplands are composed of underlying gritstone and overlying peat, then moist terrain is regularly encountered. This too has been kept to a minimum, but at the end of the day this is an integral feature of the Pennine heights.

Having explored these fells on countless occasions over half a century, it seems odd now to recall that this book was first conceived halfway through that period - though in the interests of accuracy all routes were walked in 2023. On a personal note, it was especially satisfying to complete the Three Peaks Walk as an OAP after a 17-year gap! Whilst the hills of the Dales may lack the grandeur of neighbouring Lakeland, they remain wonderful places to be. Tread carefully and savour the big landscapes in the land of the lapwing and the curlew.

Cautley Crag from the River Rawthey

Introduction

	Mountain	**Feet**	**Metres**
1	Whernside	2415	736
2	Ingleborough	2375	724
3	Great Shunner Fell	2349	716
4	High Seat	2326	709
5	Wild Boar Fell	2323	708
6	Great Whernside	2310	704
7	Buckden Pike	2303	702
8	Pen-y-ghent	2277	694
9	Great Coum	2254	687
10	Swarth Fell	2234	681
11	Plover Hill	2231	680
12	Baugh Fell	2224	678
13	The Calf	2218	676
14	Lovely Seat	2214	675
15	Calders	2211	674
16	Widdale Fell	2205	672
17	Rogan's Seat	2205	672
18	Fountains Fell	2192	668
19	Dodd Fell	2192	668
20	Lunds Fell	2188	667
21	Nine Standards Rigg	2172	662
22	Simon Fell	2133	650
23	Yockenthwaite Moor	2110	643
24	Fell Head	2100	640
25	Yarlside	2096	639
26	Gragareth	2057	627
27	Randygill Top	2047	624
28	Darnbrook Fell	2047	624
29	Wether Fell	2014	614
30	Birks Fell	2001	610
31	Middleton Fell	2000	610

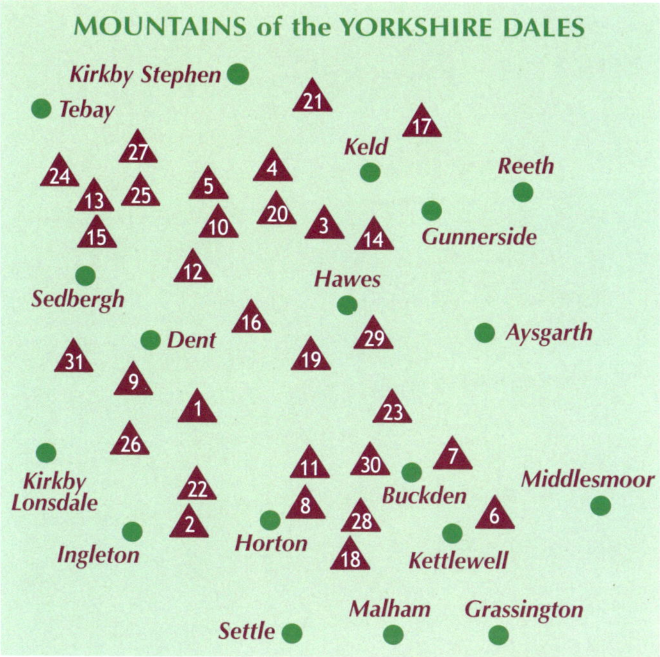

Introduction

MOUNTAINS of the YORKSHIRE DALES

The Calf from Fell Head

WALK 1 *7½ miles/1800ft from Kettlewell*

GREAT WHERNSIDE *2310ft/704m*

Start from the village centre, car park
SD 968722; BD23 5QX   Map: OL30

Great Whernside is not only Wharfedale's highest fell, it is by far the bulkiest, with easy access only from Kettlewell which it overlooks in patriarchal fashion. Eastwards, innumerable square miles of bleak moorland fall to Nidderdale, indeed the River Nidd is born within a mile of the summit. The hill's hulking ridge curves north-east to embrace 1984ft/605m Little Whernside. The south ridge broadens onto Conistone Moor, and includes popular side valleys Conistone Dib and Hebden Gill. A link with Buckden Pike is made at 1650ft/503m on the Kettlewell-Coverdale road. The summit is known as Long Crags, large tumbling boulders overlooking the western slopes, whose lower limestone reaches include caving territory. The National Park boundary shares the summit ridge with Nidderdale National Landscape (formerly AONB). Lead mining remains adorn the Wharfedale flank, while grouse shooting takes place on the eastern moors. ***From Hawkswick Moor***

GREAT WHERNSIDE • WALK 1

From the road bridge by the two hotels, head into the village along the right branch to the maypole junction, then left past the Kings Head on a narrow lane to where it turns left to bridge the beck at the far end of the village. Leave it here by keeping straight on a cart track, quickly arriving at a bridge over the sidestream of Dowber Gill. Immediately over, take a short beckside path right, rapidly escaping at a stile into the foot of a field. A path bears left up the wallside, quickly rising up the centre to a gate, then a redundant stile. Here the right path rises to level out and reveal the summit directly ahead, with a first glimpse of Hag Dyke scout centre beneath its stony escarpment.

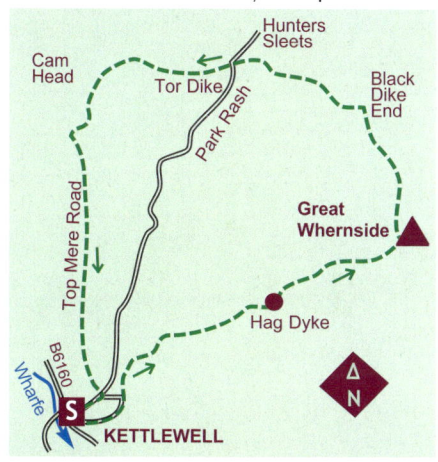

Easier going leads on to look down on the edge of the deep cleft of Dowber Gill, then rises more gently through several gates and up to meet Hag Dyke's rough access road. In the paddock, a gate to the right of the buildings put you via sheep pens onto the open fell. A path rises left to surmount the steep scarp to cairns at the top of Hag Dyke Edge: the summit now appears directly ahead. Two paths head away from these cairns, rapidly merging to commence a very slight rise across a moist shelf to the base of the upper slopes. A stone-built path enjoys a nice slant up to the right, and a continuing path makes very pleasant work of the final stretch past scattered boulders to suddenly arrive at the massive cairn and Ordnance Survey column.

The view is largely one of fells, from the nearby mass of Buckden Pike across to the distant Three Peaks, of which Pen-y-ghent appears particularly distinguished alongside Ingleborough. A short but lovely section of Wharfedale can be seen from Kilnsey Crag to Grass Woods. The fell's easternmost Dales location also offers far-reaching views across the plains to the North York Moors.

Leave by heading north along the crest on a path between the fading bouldery scarp and the nearby watershed fence. An early marker post sends a lower path angling away, but it's nicer to remain on the

WALK 1 • GREAT WHERNSIDE

Encountered on the described ascent route, **Hag Dyke** is a former farm at a heady 1509ft/460m up on a shelf beneath a bouldery escarpment. It became a scouts' outdoor centre in 1947, and its chapel in a former barn is the highest consecrated ground in the country. Today it also serves as a hostel for large groups. Dowbergill Passage (see page 16) runs at some depth directly beneath it.

GREAT WHERNSIDE • WALK 1

Looking west from Great Whernside's summit rocks

crest path. A large circular stone shelter fashioned from the plentiful rocks is passed as you approach the final rocks at Blackfell Crags: though the path is not always distinct due to the stony terrain, the way remains obvious. A splendid fenceside path continues down the broad ridge, revealing Penhill, Little Whernside and the two Nidd Head reservoirs as it levels out to reach a wall corner at Black Dike End.

Descending from Black Dike End, looking to Buckden Pike

WALK 1 • GREAT WHERNSIDE

Little Whernside from Scar House Reservoir, Upper Nidderdale

Witnessed at close hand on the return leg of the walk, **Tor Dike** is a 2000-year old defensive earthwork of the Iron Age Brigante tribe, built to deter Roman invaders. It occupies the valley head of Scale Park between Great Whernside and Buckden Pike, crossed by the Kettlewell-Coverdale road. Extending for some 1^{1}2 miles, its very distinctive ditch and rampart also take full advantage of a natural craggy escarpment.

GREAT WHERNSIDE • WALK 1

Great Whernside across the River Wharfe from Old Cote Moor

Don't cross the stile, but take the path left with the wall to drop quickly to a stile where the lower path comes in. Across it are two options, one of which avoids the worst of the public footpath's unsavoury wet section. The public footpath heads away, with a brief rough section preceding a grassy slant that soon swings downhill into the morass. It drops steadily through this to run to a gate/stile at a wall junction where the variants merge. A drier option descends alongside the wall-

Great Whernside from across Park Rash

WALK 1 • GREAT WHERNSIDE

cum-fence, steep grass giving way to largely trouble-free reeds as you drop to a wall junction at the bottom. Turning right, the short-cropped turf leads you along a limestone shelf above the wall to a re-uniting of the ways. Very distinctive here is a section of Tor Dike. The path heads away up a tiny rise with the dike's bank, then makes a short, level stroll to join the Park Rash road at a cattle-grid just this side of its summit.

Ski-mountaineering on Hag Dyke Edge

Beneath the western flank of the mountain above Kettlewell, **Providence Pot** is one of the Dales' better-known potholes. A modest manhole cover guards the vertical entrance at the head of the deep valley of Dowber Gill, which drives a narrow wedge deep into the hillside. This is the key to an underground system in which the classic but very demanding Dowbergill Passage was established in 1955 to link up with Dow Cave a mile to the north. It is interesting to note that the Providence entrance is some 250ft higher than the exit at Dow Cave, and whilst the route is largely a straight line, it involves countless amounts of up and down work.

GREAT WHERNSIDE • WALK 1

Ascending to Hag Dyke from Dowber Gill

Cross straight over and bear left on a broad, grassy way, which runs a splendid level course for some time with a wall close by on your left. Reaching a bridle-gate/stile at a wall junction, a thinner path takes over, still by the wall and contouring above it at a tumbling streamlet. Around the rear of shapely knolls you rejoin the wall to quickly reach Top Mere Gate in it. Through this a broader, level green way heads off, the walls quickly diverging before you arrive at a waymarked fork at Cam Head. Throughout all of this stage, Great Whernside's broad shoulders dominate to the left. Bear left, soon dropping gently down to a gate at a wall junction alongside sheep pens. Through this the way runs on to drop gently to become enclosed at a gate/stile. As Top Mere Road this remains your foolproof return to the village, which reveals itself dramatically at your feet towards the end. The track finally becomes stonier to emerge onto the Park Rash road on the village edge, going right to return to the centre.

Alternative ascents
- **Kettlewell** 3 miles/1750ft
  via Dowber Gill Beck, Providence Pot, Hag Dyke
- **Kettlewell** 3 miles/1650ft
  via Hag Dyke track, Hag Dyke
- **Park Rash** 1³⁄₄ miles/750ft
  via Black Dike End
- **Scar House** 6¹⁄₄ miles/1400ft
  via Lodge, Angram Pasture, Black Dike End

WALK 2 *5¼ miles/1650ft from Buckden*

BUCKDEN PIKE *2303ft/702m*

Start from the village centre, car park
SD 942772; BD23 5JA   Map: OL30

Outwith the Three Peaks this is perhaps the most popular Dales fell, with a wealth of interesting paths. Buckden Pike's form - always struggling to attain the outline of a pike - is best appreciated from the slopes of Birks Fell across the dale. The main ridge runs south at high level for some time, featuring subsidiary Tor Mere Top (2060ft/628m) before ultimately falling to Kettlewell. Western slopes drop steeply to the River Wharfe, with deep-carved gills tumbling to Buckden and Starbotton villages: Buckden Beck in particular is hugely characterful with splendid waterfalls. Here also is the best surviving of several lead mining sites around its slopes. A pair of contrasting long ridges run north-east to enclose the peaceful Walden Valley, an offshoot of Wensleydale. The eastern one retains much height and character to run out to the familiar crest of Penhill. Buckden Pike's summit bears the older name of Buckden Gavel.   *From Old Cote Moor*

BUCKDEN PIKE • WALK 2

Leave the car park by a gate at its northern end, from where a stony track makes its way gently up Buckden Rake. At once, however, double back up the grassy bank to a gate/stile in a fence pointing 'to Starbotton & Buckden Lead Mine'. The wallside path continues away, dropping to Buckden Beck as it flows over rocky slabs. Turn down as if to re-enter the village, but instead cross the beck on solid stepping-stones. A grassy track runs upstream to double back uphill away from the beck. Joining a wall it runs on as a broad path for some time, and beyond a second gate commences a raking course up the fellside. This old mine track of Eastside Road rises consistently across the colourful slope, initially steeply with a fine bird's-eye view over the village.

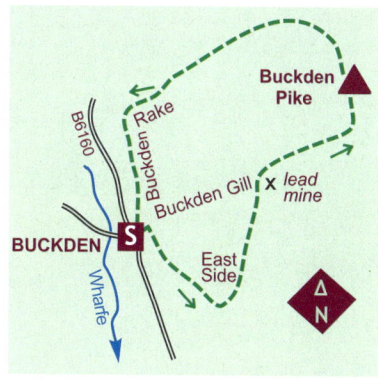

This super ascent slants all the way up the steep flank of East Side with outstanding Upper Wharfedale views. Easing out it become greener and maintains its slant across the pastures until faced by a solid boundary wall. Here it doubles back sharply left to meet the previous wall. The path rises right with this to a guidepost where it meets the former leadminers' path from Starbotton. Bear left on your main path, zigzagging uphill to reach a wall corner. It then slants above the wall across a couple of pastures, with the edge of a slight scar at the top. Through a gate above, it levels out and now a contrastingly thin trod runs on. The summit looms large seemingly far ahead. Advance on across a couple of level pastures to a stile in an outer wall corner, then along the wallside heading away. Part way on at a gateway in an old wall, as the wall drops away keep on, losing just a little height to contour around beneath steeper slopes. Dropping slightly you arrive at the decaying remains of Buckden Lead Mine, with its prominent large spoil heap and an arched level.

Resume by crossing to an old ascending wall opposite, where a clear path re-forms, rising right above the workings to a wall corner. By now Fountains Fell, Pen-y-ghent and Ingleborough have appeared to the west. The path swings right to rise more gently, meeting a wall to ease out at a wall corner on Buckden Pike's summit ridge. Big views ahead are dominated by Great Whernside, also featuring Little Whernside and Penhill. From the left-hand stile it is a two-minute stroll

WALK 2 • BUCKDEN PIKE

Thrills and spills deep inside Buckden Gill

Buckden Pike memorial cross was erected in 1973 by Polish airman Joe Fusniak, the lone survivor of an RAF Wellington bomber's crash on the summit ridge during a blizzard in January 1942. His five crewmates sadly perished, the tragedy being compounded by the fact that just a few more feet of altitude would have cleared the mountain. The memorial contains fragments of the plane and a fox's head, for it was a fox's paw-prints that aided the airman's stumbling descent with a broken ankle to reach the civilization of Cray.

BUCKDEN PIKE • WALK 2

Buckden Lead Mine at the top of Buckden Gill

on stone flags to gain the Ordnance Survey column and summit cairn. Buckden Pike's virtues as a viewpoint are in its distant prospects, which are truly extensive. Most of the major Dales' summits are on show in the western sector, with Pen-yghent and Ingleborough forming a shapely twosome. The contrastingly distant eastern horizon features the North York Moors escarpment across the Vale of Mowbray.

Horse Head Moor and Langstrothdale from the descent path above Cray

WALK 2 • BUCKDEN PIKE

Buckden Pike from Cray

Descent begins by heading north with the wall on a rebuilt path, an early steeper section being stone-pitched. After a lengthy descent by the wall the path leaves it to commence a long slant down across the fellside, allowing you to fully savour the Langstrothdale scene ahead.

The regular appendage of 'road' names to the various **green lanes** on these slopes signifies their importance in times past. Today classic walkers' highways, they originally served far more functional tasks, and both the contrasting styles of the Top Mere and Starbotton Cam Roads would be used to reach peat grounds and lead workings. Their well-laid courses were designed for easy descent with the spoils. The old road out of Starbotton was in addition on a packhorse route and drovers' road connecting Coverdale and Malham.

BUCKDEN PIKE • WALK 2

Lead workings on Tor Mere Top, looking to Little Whernside

The built path ends just short of a bridle-gate, becoming a green way through lush pastures, and passing beneath a limestone scar. The tiny hamlet of Cray is seen in its idyllic location below. This diagonal course is maintained through several old walls, with intermittently moist sections. Through a final gate it curves right down to merge into a path along Buckden Rake. Turn left through a gate and follow this superb old way all the way back into Buckden. This is one of the few confirmed sections of the Roman road that connected forts at Ilkley and Bainbridge. Initially a level green way, it swings stonily down to the left above Rakes Wood for the final stage back to the car park.

Alternative ascents

- **Buckden** 2 miles/1600ft
  *via Buckden Beck,
  Buckden Lead Mine*
- **Buckden** 2½ miles/1500ft
  via Buckden Rake
- **Cray** 2¼ miles/1250ft
- **Starbotton** 3 miles/1550ft
  *via Walden Road,
  Starbotton Fell*
- **Starbotton** 3 miles/1650ft
  via Walden Road, East Side, Buckden Lead Mine
- **Starbotton** 4 miles/1650ft
  via Starbotton Cam Road, Starbotton Out Moor
- **Kettlewell** 5 miles/1700ft *via Top Mere Rd, Cam Head, Tor Mere Top*
- **Park Rash** 3 miles/700ft *via Tor Mere Top*
- **Walden Head** 2¾ miles/1300ft *via Walden Moor*

WALK 3 *5¼ miles/1350ft from Buckden*

BIRKS FELL *2001ft/610m*

Start from the village centre, car park
SD 942772; BD23 5JA   Map: OL30

    Birks Fell was long regarded as the most innocuous of Yorkshire mountains until mapping temporarily demoted it below the magical contour: happily, a 2006 survey re-instated the qualifying spot height. This is the highest point of a mighty ridge stretching from Wharfedale to an arbitrary conclusion in Ribblesdale, though for the most part it divides Wharfedale from its offspring Littondale. An extensive tarn sits within a stone's throw of the summit. Attractive woodland and numerous potholes occupy the lower slopes above archetypal Dales villages such as Starbotton and Arncliffe. Much heather decorates the Littondale flanks, while limestone scars are abundant on the easternmost wedge of the fell above Hawkswick and Kettlewell, with lead mining remains in evidence. On the Littondale flank, Crystal Beck and Pott Beck carve deep defiles falling towards the village of Litton. *From Starbotton*

BIRKS FELL • WALK 3

From the green head down the minor road for Hawes. Not far beyond Buckden Bridge on the River Wharfe, go left on Redmire farm drive. Quickly reaching a gate/cattle-grid, ignore the drive left and take the stony bridleway zigzagging up the field. At the top left corner, gates either side of sheep pens put you onto the base of the open fell. The pleasant track slants gently left through bracken to a waymarked fork just after a small gill. Leaving the main track, rise right on the broad path to start the main climb, with the bare fell above. With occasional old marker posts, the largely very good path slants at a steady angle up the hill, ultimately steepening a little as flagstones see you up to a large cairn, the first of three neighbours. This is virtually the end of the climbing at the edge of the broad ridge-top. In poor conditions you could simply remain on this path the short way to the ridge-wall.

Ideally, head away right with the vestiges of a wall from the third cairn, and a trod quickly becomes clearer to run parallel to its left. This runs for some time, rising only ever slightly until lonely Birks Tarn appears ahead with Pen-y-ghent's top beyond. Passing nearest the tarn at

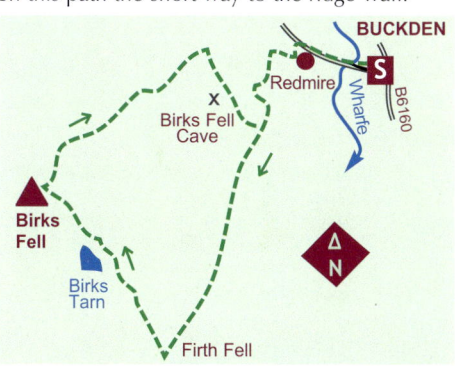

its far end the trod forge on, still near the old wall until veering briefly left up a slope to gain the summit cairn. Best feature of the view looks south to Fountains Fell, the Bowland moors and the nearby Three Peaks. In the other direction, sprawling neighbours Yockenthwaite Moor, Buckden Pike and Great Whernside inevitably dominate.

Though a thin trod runs to the very wall corner, the descent route simply crosses to the nearest wall, where turn right on a faint trod. Initially easy going, the wall drops away to arrive at a briefly steeper section at Low Combe Stoop: note the quality of the craftsman-built wall here. Wind cautiously down, soon easing to feel you're already pretty much down. Remain near the wall all the way, encountering moister ground and passing a couple of tiny conifer stands, utilising a quad track. As the wall is replaced by a fence near the moister bottom, omit the very corner by veering right past an outer fence corner to approach the intake wall just below.

WALK 3 • BIRKS FELL

Turn right on much firmer ground, passing a low limestone shelf on your right and a fenced enclosure by the wall: a super green track rapidly forms parallel with the nearby wall below. Through bracken it passes within 100 yards of Birks Fell Cave at a modest limestone ravine

Birks Fell marks the high point of the **Horse Head Ridge**, which boasts an unprecedented array of minor tops forming insignificant rises. From west to east these are: Cosh Knott (1965ft/599m), High Greenfield Knott (1975ft/602m), Horse Head (1985ft/605m), Sugar Loaf (1998ft/609m), Moss Top (1978ft/603m), Birks Fell itself, and Firth Fell (1991ft/607m). The ridge is also unique in being crossed by numerous inter-valley paths linking villages and hamlets in Wharfedale and Littondale. These include Horse Head Pass and the popular Old Cote Moor and Hawkswick Moor routes.

BIRKS FELL • WALK 3

Birks Tarn

Birks Fell across Littondale
Opposite: Buckden Pike from Birks Fell Cave

just above. The chirpy beck flows from the moors down through the rocks to sink in the cave itself. The track runs on to a scant ruin (with a stone shooting cabin a little higher), where drop briefly left back onto the outward track two minutes above the sheep pens.

> ### Alternative ascents
> - **Litton** 2¾ miles/1200ft
>   *via Middle Moor, Moss Top*
> - **Litton** 2¾ miles/1250ft
>   *via Ackerley Moor, Firth Fell*
> - **Halton Gill** 3¾ miles/1150ft
>   *via Horse Head Gate, Horse Head Moor, Moss Top*
> - **Raisgill** 3¾ miles/1250ft
>   *via Horse Head Gate, Horse Head Moor, Moss Top*

WALK 4   *7 miles/1500ft from Hubberholme*

YOCKENTHWAITE MOOR *2110ft/643m*

Start from the hamlet centre, riverbank parking over bridge near church   SD 926782; BD23 5JE   Map: OL30

Travellers reaching the upper limits of Wharfedale beyond Hubberholme are faced with a great moorland barrier that seems to bar any exit from the dalehead. This is Yockenthwaite Moor – also known as Middle Tongue - a vast tract of upland that divides Langstrothdale from Wensleydale's offshoot Raydale. The fell can be said to stretch from the Buckden-Hawes road on Fleet Moss to the Buckden-Aysgarth road over Kidstones, extending for some miles at a lofty, scarcely varying altitude. Spread along this broad, spongy ridge are several seldom-visited tarns. The lower flanks above the popular area around Buckden and Hubberholme form a startling contrast, for a near unbroken limestone escarpment runs from Cray to above Yockenthwaite, immediately below which are belts of rich and very old woodland.

From Raisgill

YOCKENTHWAITE MOOR • WALK 4

From a gate between church and farm, a driveway climbs towards Scar House: leave it at once on a firm path to the riverbank. This mile and a half upstream to Yockenthwaite is clear throughout, not straying more than a few strides from the Wharfe. A bonus feature is the crossing of Strans Gill's limestone ravine. The finest section is tight by the river with its low falls. Back into the fields, as Yockenthwaite appears ahead rise slightly to a gate, then straight on by the river through a gateway. At the end turn up to a corner stile in front of the first building, then through gates above the buildings to enter the green in this farming hamlet.

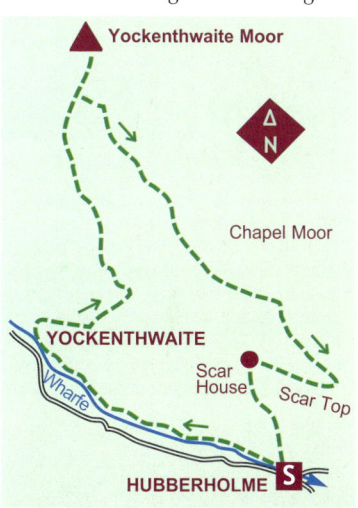

Don't drop down to the attractive arched bridge, but take the stony track up the left side of the farm. Ignore a right branch to the house behind, and take the track curving up the steep pasture to bear right, becoming stonier again as it climbs by a wall enclosing a wood. Ignoring a branch path into the trees, continue a steep pull to level out at a barn. From a kissing-gate near a gate in the fence in front, you enter the open fell. Remain on the improving track as it rises briefly with the wall, which soon turns sharp right to leave your track slanting up the grassy fell. It climbs to then swing left and rise to virtually terminate on a grassy shelf, with a shapely escarpment up above. The track resurrects briefly as it runs left to slant up again onto a larger grassy shelf before fading. Simply ascend to the obvious gap between intriguing rock formations above.

Resuming, another skyline awaits, so rise slightly left to avoid reedier ground, and up between shakeholes. Easing ground leads to a massive fenced enclosure, with a quad track along its near side. Pass left of this on a trod to the top corner, and resume a gentle rise with an intermittent trod. Look back to see Fountains Fell, Pen-y-ghent and Plover Hill joining Ingleborough above the Horse Head ridge. Rapidly levelling, ahead now is the watershed, just beneath which pick out your objective of a stone hut. A short way on, you meet a broad, grassy channel: bear left up this, narrowing to a trod to join a grassy quad

WALK 4 • YOCKENTHWAITE MOOR

track. Turning right for a level spell, when nearest to the hut leave the track and cross the 150 moist yards to it. Rise behind it onto a brow to see the Ordnance Survey column just minutes across the peat, with the watershed fence behind it. The superb all-round panorama is very much an upland one, with rolling moorland stretching as far as the eye can see. Virtually all of the Dales fells feature, with Fell Head in the Howgills possibly the only omission. Additionally, the Bowland moors, South Lakeland fells and North Pennines are seen more distantly.

Commence the return by returning to the hut, then back to the track. This time go left, quickly swinging right to drop gently away to approach the fenced enclosure's opposite corner. Go left a few strides to the corner itself, then the track drops to a corner just below. Here leave it as it drops right outside the fence, and instead slant gently left

YOCKENTHWAITE MOOR • WALK 4

The stone hut beneath the summit

Opposite: Crook Gill above Cray

Oughtershaw Tarn on the broad plateau west of the summit

down the pathless slope on improving terrain. Briefly with a streamlet, slant further left down to a gate where a fenced enclosure meets a descending wall. Through it turn down the wallside on a steady grassy way down the slopes of Chapel Fell.

Just before a fence replaces the wall, bear gently left on a poor quad track through reeds. This fades to briefly continue as a fading trod on better ground. Maintain this slant the short way down to a grassy plateau near an old sheepfold. Now bear left along the shelf, crossing to limestone outcrops at the start of a very modest escarpment. Go left along this minor edge with a parallel wall not far below. Sheeptrods lead along to the second, broader half on short-cropped grass to reach a minor nick. Drop down the tractor track here, slanting more faintly left down to the top of a pronounced brow of substantial tumbled boulders.

The sunken track drops to a gate in the wall below, with a labyrinth of stone folds on your left. Bear left down this rough pasture, and as a modest grassy way fades, drop more directly down improving terrain onto a level grass track. With super views down Wharfedale's deep trough go left towards the wall, turning down its near side to drop pleasantly to a public footpath at a stile. Turn right for a super stroll above Scar Top's wooded scarp, soon arriving above isolated Scar House. Drop between the buildings and down the access road into Hubberholme.

Alternative ascents
- **Kidstones Pass**
  3¾ miles/800ft
  via The Stake, Chapel Moor
- **Stalling Busk**
  4½ miles/1050ft
  via The Stake, South Grain Tarn

31

WALK 5

5¾ miles/1000ft from Rainscar

FOUNTAINS FELL
DARNBROOK FELL

2192ft/668m
2047ft/624m

Start from junction with unsurfaced road ¾-mile to north towards Halton Gill SD 855728; BD24 9PW   Map: OL30

Fountains Fell is a large upland sat between Pen-y-ghent and the delights of Malham Tarn. Its higher reaches are dotted with mining remains, for both coal and lead were won here. The colliery was at its peak in the early 19th century, your ascent route being the old colliers' way. The Pennine Way traverses the hill, while a subsidiary South Top stands at 2172ft/662m beyond the extensive Fountains Fell Tarn. Named from the Cistercian monks of Fountains Abbey, these wealthy landowners held vast sheep runs across swathes of the Dales. Lonely Darnbrook Fell skulks in Fountains' shadow, and is named from an ancient farmstead sheltering under its eastern flank. The most interesting aspect is the wooded lower slopes above the Skirfare in Littondale between Litton and Arncliffe. The western flank also falls to lovely surrounds, where limestone scars fall to the colourful ravine of Pen-y-ghent Gill.   *From Pen-y-ghent*

FOUNTAINS FELL & DARNBROOK FELL • WALK 5

Head south along the road's open verges, with Fountains Fell to your left and majestic Pen-y-ghent to your right. Rising a little, it quickly arrives at a cattle-grid where you meet the Pennine Way. Follow its path left up the near side of the sturdy wall, soon passing through an intervening bridle-gate. A little above a modest limestone scar (by which time Ingleborough has appeared beyond Pen-y-ghent), the path swings left to commence a super slant across the flank. Tracing a grooved colliers' way all the way to the summit plateau, it passes beneath modest crags then swings right onto the felltop. Passing spoil heaps you quickly cross to a stile in the ridge-wall just ahead. The summit cairn is visible over to the right, with only a tiny amount of uphill to gain it.

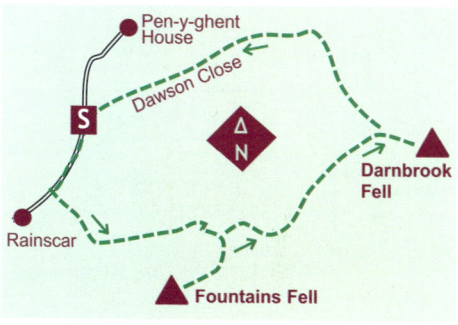

Beyond the stile be aware of the presence of some old and very deep mineshafts, though happily they should be safely fenced. Immediately on the left is a tiny shaft, with a large cairn and two lesser ones on a landscape of spoil heaps and hummocks. The Pennine Way heads away gently right, but after 120 yards take the second lesser but very clear path branching right just as the main path prepares to drop gently away. Almost at once you pass a major shaft, and just yards further is a stone hut known as the 'Igloo', erected by miners as a coke oven. A little beyond it you reach a fork: the branches rejoin just before the summit. The left one rises gently to pass another major shaft, while the right one winds around to their junction just short of the summit cairn.

The cairn isn't what it once was, but still offers a magnificent panorama. Finest feature is neighbouring Peny-ghent, with Ingleborough slotting in nicely behind it. The hill's southerly location makes it a good vantage point for a wealth of lower-lying hill country, with the following all featuring in a clockwise direction: Grassington Moor, Parson's Pulpit, Simon's Seat, Barden Moor, Skipton Moor, Rombalds Moor, Rye Loaf Hill, Pendle Hill, Grindleton Fell, then the Bowland moors featuring White Hill and Bowland's highest point, Ward's Stone. Interestingly, Whernside and Wild Boar Fell are visible from the Pennine Way path but hidden from the summit view.

WALK 5 • FOUNTAINS FELL & DARNBROOK FELL

Fountains Fell Tarn

For the transfer to Darnbrook Fell, first retrace steps to the wall-stile. Don't cross but turn down its near side, with the peaty dome of Darnbrook Fell currently dwarfed by the more distant Buckden Pike. A thin trod drops to quickly reach an inner corner, going right with the wall to quickly resume downhill with an intermittent quad track. Soon reaching a gate in it just yards short of a wall junction, cross to resume on the wall's left side. This will remain your guide to within five minutes of the summit. With Halton Gill appearing on the floor of Littondale it drops gently to a flat, moist saddle, across which the trod makes an excellent job of a very gentle ascent to run to a wall corner. Through the gate on the right, a fence leads gently away up to the final stage: trods run on both sides, with barb-free crossings either at the outset or 50 yards short of the summit. A slight, moist rise passes a short walled section to rapidly level to reveal the Ordnance Survey column just

Mine workings north of Fountains Fell summit

FOUNTAINS FELL & DARNBROOK FELL • WALK 5

The 'Igloo' on Fountains Fell

Darnbrook Fell summit

ahead. The second barb-free section sees the trods merge for the final fifty yards. The trig point stands forlornly and stubbornly amid eroded peat revealing its substantial foundations.

Leave by returning to the gate at the wall corner, and set off on the simplest of descents with the wall on your right. For the most part a quad track drops steadily and very pleasantly, allowing you to enjoy a superb panorama featuring Pen-y-ghent and upper Littondale. Lower down, the track splinters amid moister terrain: simply remain near the wall down to a gate at a junction with a wall from the left. Through it head away to a minor brow revealing the old unmade road from Litton just two minutes below. Drop to join it alongside a gate, and turn left for a splendid conclusion as it crosses the lush terrain of Dawson Close. Virtually level and largely grassy, it encounters several streams and gates to lead unfailingly back to the start.

Alternative ascents

Fountains Fell
- **Tennant Gill**
  2¾ miles/950ft
  via Pennine Way

Darnbrook Fell
- **Giant's Grave**
  2¼ miles/700ft
  via Dawson Close
- **Litton** 3 miles/1250ft
  *via New Bridge,
  Dawson Close Road*

35

WALK 6 *8¾ miles/1750ft from Horton-in-Ribblesdale*

PEN-Y-GHENT
PLOVER HILL

2277ft/694m
2231ft/680m

Start from the village centre, car park
SD 808726; BD24 0HF   Map: OL2

The Lion of Ribblesdale is a magnificent mountain that begs to be climbed, thanks to its aggressive profile hovering over Horton. The ascent of the distinctive south ridge is possibly more trodden than any path on the Dales hills, and the only one that requires moments of hands on rock. The tiers of limestone and gritstone encountered fan out along the flanks, with the gleaming limestone band featuring the detached pillar of Pen-y-ghent Pinnacle. Famous potholes on its western flank are Hull Pot and Hunt Pot, the latter a tiny but deep slit in contrast to its mighty neighbour. The name derives from the Celtic 'Hill of the Winds' or the Welsh 'Hill on the Border'. Named from an iconic bird of the uplands, neighbouring but unsung Plover Hill looks almost entirely over Littondale's bleak upper reaches, where it claims a major stake in the fine limestone valley of Pen-y-ghent Gill.   *From above Brackenbottom*

PEN-Y-GHENT & PLOVER HILL • WALK 6

Pen-y-ghent dominates Horton, looking tall and daunting at the outset. From the car park head south along the street past the Pen-y-ghent Café, and just after the campsite (but before the church), a small gate on the left sends a tarmac path along a fieldside. Through a small gate at the end the path drops down steps between houses onto a back lane. Go briefly left and cross a footbridge on Douk Gill, then left on a parallel back lane. This passes the former school and winds around above the beck to the hamlet of Brackenbottom.

Before the first building take a gate on the left, with a bridle-gate up above it. This sends a built path steeply up a fieldside, remaining with the wall for the entire first half of the climb. Views over the village see Ingleborough rising high above Horton's massive quarry. On nearing a bridle-gate the gradient eases and the hill's magnificent profile

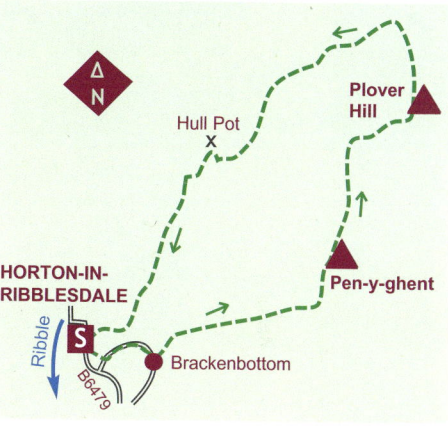

returns, a quite inspirational objective. Two further bridle-gates in cross-walls are met, the path being largely stone-flagged or on firm chippings. Modest bands of limestone and a couple of level sections feature, while the mountain's profile grows in authority. The climb's major turning point comes as you rise to a bridle-gate at the foot of the south ridge, and earn views eastwards to Fountains Fell.

The gate sends a broad path left up the wallside for the big push, firstly alongside and up the edge of a limestone band featuring natural steps. This quickly puts you onto a shelf beneath a sprawling gritstone boulderfield. Again the path runs to the right side, then clambers up between them to engage hands to scale the gritstone band. Beyond this you are virtually on the top, and a simple stroll on a stone-flagged path leads up to gain the Ordnance Survey column and modern shelter. Pen-y-ghent's summit is a grand place to be, with extensive views over Three Peaks country and far beyond: Ingleborough's massif inevitably takes precedence. Lancashire's Pendle Hill and the sprawling Bowland moors fill a large area to the south.

WALK 6 • PEN-Y-GHENT & PLOVER HILL

Pen-y-ghent from Overdale, on the long ridge south to Stainforth

Through either of the stiles ignore the main path heading away, and take a more inviting one heading north with the wall towards Plover Hill's broad moorland dome. Part way down the pleasant descent to the saddle you can locate Pen-y-ghent's impressive limestone

Hull Pot is a remarkable chasm of sheer limestone walls in the lap of Pen-y-ghent, some 300 feet long and 60 feet wide. It is seen at its very best when Hull Pot Beck plunges over the northern edge: under normal conditions it will have sunk underground before reaching the rim. On extreme occasions, it has been known to fill completely.

PEN-Y-GHENT & PLOVER HILL • WALK 6

At the foot of the clamber up Pen-y-ghent's south ridge

pinnacle down to the left, looking very distinct for a few brief yards. Across the modestly bouldery saddle, a corner wall-stile precedes a simple ascent close by the wall. At times moist and later peaty, a broader path keeps its distance from the wall, while an intermittent thinner one stays with it. On the final stage the path runs pleasantly to a ladder-stile on a wall junction. This gives access to the felltop but not the actual summit at this curious alignment of walls. From the stile the

Walkers descending the south ridge

WALK 6 • PEN-Y-GHENT & PLOVER HILL

Heading for Plover Hill from Pen-y-ghent

summit cairn is seen hovering above a small, stony hollow over the wall to your right. As it can only be a foot or so higher than where you are, there seems little justification, other than to purists, for having to twice scale the substantial wall.

Pen-y-ghent from Sulber limestone pavements, under Simon Fell

PEN-Y-GHENT & PLOVER HILL • WALK 6

Pen-y-ghent's eastern flank from Dawson Close, under Fountains Fell

Leave by a broad, grassy path bearing left across open ground from the ladder-stile. Quickly becoming well-worn, it slants down the fellside to meet a wall, becoming stone-pitched at this point. A very pleasing sense of remoteness pervades hereabouts, with a glimpse of Foxup at the head of Littondale. The path now makes an intriguing, steep descent between craggy flanks, then drops pleasantly and gently

Descending Horton Scar Lane back into Horton-in-Ribblesdale

WALK 6 • PEN-Y-GHENT & PLOVER HILL

Snowdrifts on the summit of Plover Hill

onto the broad, grassy track of Foxup Road. Turn left to commence a splendid prolonged stride, largely level and lush underfoot amid what is otherwise rough terrain. Through several gates, and later with an adjacent wall, Pen-y-ghent's classic profile returns. After ultimately shaking off the wall, the path drops gently down and swings right to a wall, across which is the sudden, dramatic appearance of Hull Pot. The now broader way passes through a gate just along to the left, through which a thinner path runs 100 yards right to Hull Pot. You'll quickly appreciate this is no place for skylarking about!

On the Pen-y-ghent-Plover Hill ridge, looking to Ingleborough

PEN-Y-GHENT & PLOVER HILL • WALK 6

45699 Galatea steams up Ribblesdale beneath Pen-y-ghent

Leave on a broad, grassy way running left through a gentle trough the five minutes to a gate at the head of Horton Scar Lane. Through it simply follow the rough, walled track all the way down to the village, enjoying views across to Pen-y-ghent's familiar profile and far over the valley. When Horton's houses are just ahead, keep right at a fork to alight onto the street just along from the Pen-y-ghent Café.

Alternative ascents

Pen-y-ghent
- **Horton** 3½ miles/1550ft
  via Horton Scar Lane, Hull Pot
- **Helwith Bridge** 3½ miles/1650ft
  via Long Lane, Churn Milk Hole
- **Stainforth** 4¼ miles/1700ft
  *via Great Moor Head,
  Overdale, Churn Milk Hole*
- **Dale Head** 1¾ miles/900ft
  via Churn Milk Hole

Plover Hill
- **Horton** 4½ miles/1550ft *via Horton Scar Lane, Hull Pot, Foxup Moor*
- **Giant's Grave** 1½ miles/950ft *via Lockey Beck*
- **Halton Gill** 3½ miles/1350ft *via Foxup, Foxup Moor*

WALK 7   10¾ miles/2200ft from Clapham

INGLEBOROUGH   *2375ft/724m*
SIMON FELL   *2133ft/650m*

Start from the village centre, car park
SD 745692; LA2 8EQ   Map: OL2

The most famous mountain in the Pennines, and a favourite of all Yorkshiremen (and women), Ingleborough is a captivating hill. The gently tilted summit plateau is recognizable from near and far, with the steep western slopes creating the finest aspect. The upland triangle of its vast massif includes Simon Fell to the north, while sprawling southern slopes fall to dramatic limestone landscapes which include the uplands of Moughton and Norber: the latter is famous for its erratic Silurian boulders resting on limestone pedestals. Caves and potholes on the hill's immediate slopes include not only Gaping Gill, Ingleborough Cave and White Scar Cave, but a host of others known by the caving fraternity, with many on the innocuous looking Newby Moss. Limestone pavements also feature strongly at mid height all around the hill, much of these being within a National Nature Reserve.   *From Scales Moor*

INGLEBOROUGH & SIMON FELL • WALK 7

From the car park cross the road to a stone-arched footbridge and take the road right. As it turns left, pass through a gateway in front where a ticket machine collects modest dues for entering the private grounds beyond. Note that this (but also Clapdale's charms) can be avoided by going left on the road 100 yards to turn right up a walled access track. This leads unfailingly to Clapdale Farm: passing straight through the yard and into the pasture behind, a path drops right to a gate onto the main route in Clapdale.

For the highly recommended approach through the valley of Clapdale, however, a track zigzags up to the foot of an extensive, attractively wooded lake. This broad carriageway now runs the length of the charming estate grounds, and climbs away from the lake, high above the beck to the 18th century Grotto. A short way beyond it you emerge into the open, upper reaches of Clapdale, and the drive shadows Clapham Beck the short way to Ingleborough Cave, with guided tours and light refreshments. Just past it, a stone-arched bridge crosses the beck within yards of its resurgance at Beck Head.

Over the bridge, advance straight on through a gate/stile and along a dry trough between low limestone scars. A corner is rounded to pass through a gate/stile revealing Trow Gill, and the path undertakes an enjoyable climb through this magnificent overhanging ravine. Emerging at the top onto open moor, Little Ingleborough is quickly revealed, soon joined by Ingleborough itself. The path accompanies a wall, ignoring a ladder-stile and continuing on to reach twin wall-stiles: Ingleborough is now fully revealed. Just across the wall is the massive hollow of Bar Pot, a cavers' route into the Gaping Gill system. The path heads off across the flat moor, initially still on limestone terrain. Bearing right, within a few minutes a fork is reached, and the main right branch runs the very short way to the unmistakable hollow that is Gaping Gill. It will be immediately clear that this is no place for skylarking!

45

WALK 7 • INGLEBOROUGH & SIMON FELL

On the open moor in the lap of Ingleborough, the mighty chasm of **Gaping Gill** cannot fail to impress. The innocuous Fell Beck suddenly plunges more than 330ft/100m onto the floor of the chamber, said to be of sufficient size to hold York Minster. Over the Spring Bank and late Summer Bank Holiday weeks, local caving clubs set up a chair and winch in order to lower paying visitors into the depths, from where several miles of passages radiate. To enjoy this unique and popular experience, it's well worth making an early start from Clapham.

INGLEBOROUGH & SIMON FELL • WALK 7

Ascending through the ravine of Trow Gill

Ingleborough awaits, so just yards from the hole, take a link path to rejoin the direct one. This rises steadily then increasingly steeply towards Little Ingleborough, with a variety of built surfaces. Pen-y-ghent quickly appears behind you, with Simon Fell just across to your right. Almost at the top a large cairn and scattered rocks precede arrival on Little Ingleborough, marked by a cairn and old shelter: the climbing is almost done. The main peak now re-appears, and a firm continuation along this broad shoulder leads to a steady rise, then a slant up to a cairn on the edge of the summit plateau (ignore a continuing path around the edge). Bear left up the slightly tilted plateau to the summit, which in poor visibility can bring navigational problems – more so on leaving the top. Rising across it, however, the summit shelter should appear within a few yards, and will be reached in a couple of minutes.

Ingleborough from Little Ingleborough

WALK 7 • INGLEBOROUGH & SIMON FELL

Until recently shown on maps as Ingleborough Hill, **Ingleborough's summit** is a place of much interest. The highest ground is occupied by a four-square wind shelter with plentiful seating incorporating a view indicator; an Ordnance Survey column; a massive, sprawling cairn between the two; and a great pile of stones nearer the Ingleton edge. The latter item is the ruins of a 'hospice', erected in 1830 and largely destroyed at the same time due to the drunken revelries of those celebrating its construction! Crumbling walls around the rim of the plateau and the bases of several hut circles within were long thought to be the remains of a 2000-year old Iron Age hill-fort of the Brigante tribe, but more recent thinking is that they belong to a much older, possibly Bronze Age site.

INGLEBOROUGH & SIMON FELL • WALK 7

Looking to Simon Fell on the descent of Swine Tail from Ingleborough

As a viewpoint Ingleborough ranks superlatives, with interest in all directions. Its position as a corner-stone of the Dales guarantees great variety of scenery. 'Inland' is a skyline of rolling tops slotted in between colleagues Pen-y-ghent and Whernside, while far to the west are the Lakeland Fells. Southwards are the Bowland moors across the Wenning Valley, while Morecambe Bay glistens beyond Arnside Knott.

Ingleborough from Simon Fell

49

WALK 7 • INGLEBOROUGH & SIMON FELL

Clapdale is a beautiful distraction en route to or from Ingleborough, its grounds and lake created by the Farrer family of Ingleborough Hall in the 19th century. Botanist Reginald Farrer brought back alpine plants here from his journeys to far-flung parts. The dark tunnels at the end of the walk run beneath routes into the grounds from the hall. Alongside Ingleborough Cave, the stream emerging at Beck Head last saw daylight as Fell Beck, plunging into Gaping Gill: a connection by cavers was only established in the 1980s after many years' efforts.

INGLEBOROUGH & SIMON FELL • WALK 7

Ingleborough from Crina Bottom, on the Ingleton ascent path

Return to the plateau edge by bearing further left than your approach route, again only with hints of a path as you reach a large cairn just short of the north-east corner: in poor weather aim briefly north to the nearby defined plateau edge, then turn right along the rim to the corner. Here a steep, built path slants right down through Swine Tail's scattered boulders, becoming flagged at a cairn just yards before an upright stone. Ignore a right branch here and continue down the now fully stone-flagged path to a kissing-gate at a wall/fence junction.

Ingleborough icons:
Norber Boulders, Norber

Harryhorse Stone,
Newby Moss

51

WALK 7 • INGLEBOROUGH & SIMON FELL

Passing through, ignore the main path going left, and remain with the wall on your right over a streamlet, aiming for the innocuous Simon Fell. A largely broad way runs through a minor col and traces the wall past a kink to rise gently and quickly to the summit. The tiniest of cairns stands just out from the wall. The view is inevitably not too dissimilar to that of its neighbour, though Simon Fell does of course have the advantage of a super prospect of mighty Ingleborough itself!

Ingleborough and Simon Fell from Moughton Scars

Leave by resuming with the wall down a more defined short drop to a ladder-stile in the wall corner below. Across, go right on a thin trod with the wall, gaining a small amount of height as it winds pleasantly around through easy limestone terrain. Reaching a corner remain with the wall going right, quickly dropping to moister terrain. Here a short but horribly soggy shelf has to be crossed: circumventing it further right is perhaps the best option before a quad track appears and drops down near the wall, pleasantly again to meet the Horton path. For a shorter option, simply cross over this and down the continuing track, with the wall over to the left to drop unfailingly back to Gaping Gill.

The full route turns left over the wall-stile, and the broad path drops steadily away. Joined by a wall, you drop to a ruinous shooting box at Juniper Gulf. A little beyond that the adjacent stream is forded to a bridle-gate/gate. 150 yards beyond that is a fork, where leave the main path for a branch right. This rapidly transforms into a super green

INGLEBOROUGH & SIMON FELL • WALK 7

way. Initially with a wall to the right, it diverges for a lengthy, effortless stroll across the bare, level moor. A limestone area is reached, passing through minor cuttings by limestone pavements. Emerging, it runs on above a large limestone pavement to the left, and along to meet the broader Horton-Clapham path.

Go right, ignoring an immediate left branch and quickly on to a fork at Long Scar with a landmark cairn on the knoll ahead. Either will suffice: the left is shorter, while the right winds around the knoll to run back left above an upland basin to merge above a wall corner. Though united they drop in curious tandem to a gate in a wall below, then slanting down to a gate in a wall to the left: Trow Gill is just in front. This is the head of Long Lane, which will lead unfailingly back parallel with Clapdale just below. There are two opportunities to re-enter Clapdale and return through the estate (more interesting than Long Lane): first is an early ladder-stile where drop to one just below onto the track; or much further is a wall-stile level with Clapdale Farm, sending a wallside path down to a footbridge by the estate entrance. Long Lane meanwhile ultimately arrives at a T-junction, where go right to drop steeply and roughly beneath two dark tunnels to emerge back into the village alongside the church.

Alternative ascents

Ingleborough
- **Ingleton**
  $3^1{}_2$ miles/2000ft
  via Crina Bottom
- **Horton** $4^3{}_4$ miles/1750ft
  *via Sulber Nick,
  Simon Fell Breast*
- **Chapel-le-Dale**
  $2^1{}_2$ miles/1450ft
  *via Southerscales,
  Humphrey Bottom*
- **Ribblehead** $4^1{}_2$ miles/1650ft *via Colt Park, Park Fell*
- **Newby** $3^1{}_2$ miles/1850ft *via Newby Moss, Little Ingleborough*
- **Cold Cotes** $3^1{}_4$ miles/1700ft *via Grey Scars, Little Ingleborough*
- **Austwick** $5^1{}_2$ miles/2050ft *via Crummack, Long Scar, Simon Fell Breast*

Simon Fell
- **Chapel-le-Dale** $2^1{}_2$ miles/1250ft
  via Southerscales, Humphrey Bottom
- **Ribblehead** $3^1{}_2$ miles/1400ft *via Colt Park, Park Fell*
- **Horton** $4^1{}_4$ miles/1500ft *via Sulber Nick*
- **Austwick** $5^1{}_4$ miles/1800ft *via Crummack, Long Scar*

WALK 8 *8 miles/1600ft from Ribblehead*

WHERNSIDE *2415ft/736m*

Start from B6255/B6479 junction just north of pub, large lay-bys SD 764792; LA6 3AS Map: OL2

The crown of the Yorkshire Dales is the highest point in England south of the rugged Coniston Fells in Lakeland. Despite its status, its appearance does not rival that of its Three Peaks colleagues, though its immensity is not in question. This long, whaleback ridge has a broad western shoulder falling towards Kingsdale and a steep eastern flank dropping to Ribblehead. Northwards the ridge broadens to a shelf supporting extensive tarns before falling to Dentdale. Southwards, the ridge narrows to an extremely long wedge high above Ingleton's celebrated waterfalls: here rock climbers frequent extensive Twisleton Scars, above which similarly extensive limestone pavements occupy the shelf of Scales Moor. A further tarn, Greensett, sits on a lower shelf beneath the steep eastern flank. The hill's name derives from 'quern' - quarried stone made into millstones. *From Ingleborough*

WHERNSIDE • WALK 8

From the road junction a path runs along to meet the broad track heading for the viaduct from the pub. Already, as for most of the walk, all Three Peaks are well displayed. Just before its arches, branch right on a clear path which makes a brief pull to then shadow the railway. It runs by the iconic signal box at Bleamoor Sidings before straying a little from the line, running to a footbridge on Little Dale Beck before tracing Force Gill the short way to an aqueduct just short of Blea Moor Tunnel. Across the aqueduct the reconstructed path rises to a gate in a fence above the tunnel entrance. This yields a good view of Force Gill's splendid waterfall. The path runs left to commence the ascent proper, with a fence replacing the wall on your left. The summit ridge returns to view, and at a stile in the fence, leave the packhorse route of the Craven Way and cross to resume on the main path.

The restored path climbs more steadily to meet a fence and old wall just before landing on a broad shelf. The path then slants left with the fence/wall to cross a streamlet before the onset of a long series of stone flags again cut a corner of the fence/wall. The sizeable Greensett Tarn soon appears to your left in Whernside's lap. The flags climb to rejoin the fence/wall on the northern extremity of Whernside's mighty summit ridge, and the finest section now sees the path traverse the

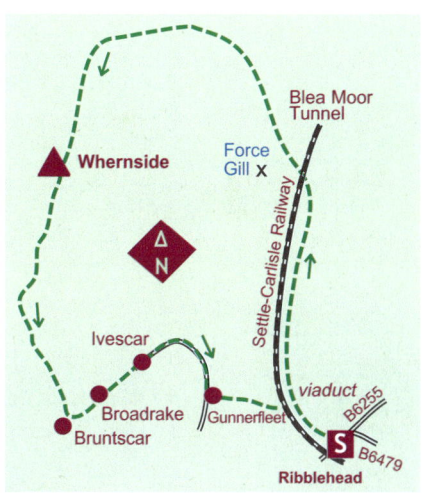

crest of the increasingly steep eastern plunge. Looking back, the Howgill Fells take their place in an expanding view, with the green floor of Dentdale appearing. A clear day brings the Lakeland Fells into place far beyond, while contrastingly closer, Whernside Tarns are seen on the plateau to the north. Only a little more effort is needed to gain the summit, which is reached by increasingly easy and enjoyable walking. The now intact wall shadows the final stage grandly along to a modern shelter, with the Ordnance Survey column found through a stile in a kink of the wall.

WALK 8 • WHERNSIDE

Ribblehead Viaduct strides boldly across the landscape at the foot of Whernside, set back from the junction of two important Dales roads beneath the isolated Station Inn. It is the Settle-Carlisle Railway that earned national fame for Ribblehead, in the shape of its 24-arch viaduct. More properly Batty Moss Viaduct, this symbol of Victorian enterprise was completed in 1875, and also became the symbol of a successful campaign to prevent closure of the line in the 1980s. During the construction years, Batty Green, as the area was known, was home to shanty towns that housed workers and their families. With names such as Sebastopol and Jericho, facilities included schools, chapels, inns and shops. Lawlessness was rife, as, sadly, was smallpox, which caused more deaths than construction accidents. Most victims were buried at nearby Chapel-le-Dale. Various grass-covered earthworks survive, including the course of tramways that brought quarried stone from Little Dale to the viaduct site.

WHERNSIDE • WALK 8

Looking down on Greensett Tarn from Whernside's north ridge

This being the highest fell in the Dales and thus this book, the panorama is inevitably quite magnificent. Eastwards is a sweeping Dales landscape of brown, rolling fells, and to the west the Gragareth-Great Coum ridge is laid out in its entirety. Pen-y-ghent rises beyond Ribblehead Viaduct, but mighty Ingleborough earns the accolades across the limestone scars of Chapel-le-Dale. In the other direction, Dentdale leads the eye to the Howgill Fells, while further west is a full complement of Lakeland Fells from Coniston Old Man to Blencathra.

Approaching Whernside's summit from the north ridge

WALK 8 • WHERNSIDE

Ingleborough from the descent to Bruntscar

Resume on the broad and stony wallside path dropping steadily away, quickly passing through a kissing-gate as the wall makes a brief dog-leg before returning. Continue for some time before two short, stone-pitched drops. At the foot of the second, the path bears left off the ridge to commence a rapid descent to the valley. The initially steep, pitched path drops to a bridle-gate in a wall, below which a better graded, often stone-flagged way affords easier progress. This longer section drops to another gate, below which a final pasture is crossed to

Whernside from Bleamoor Sidings

WHERNSIDE • WALK 8

Thornton Force on the River Twiss in the Ingleton Glens

a gate at the far corner beyond limestone outcrops. Drop a few yards towards Bruntscar then take a bridle-gate on the left alongside a barn, from where a firm path crosses a field to Broadrake with its adjoining bunkhouse. Go straight ahead to pass right of the buildings, the path resuming across successive fields linked by gates. Broadening into a grassy cart track beneath a lone house, you reach a gate into Ivescar's farmyard. Advance straight through, and out on its enclosed, surfaced access road. Swinging right at a sharp bend, it doubles back to run alongside Winterscales Beck to Gunnerfleet. Cross the bridge on the left and along a firm track past the farm buildings: immediately both the viaduct and Pen-y-ghent return to view. The track emerges from a field to run through open terrain and under the viaduct to finish as you began. Beneath the viaduct is a monument celebrating its restoration.

Alternative ascents
- **Chapel-le-Dale**
  2¾ miles/1550ft
  via Bruntscar
- **Ingleton** 6½ miles/2100ft
  via Twisleton Hall,
  Ewes Top, West Fell
- **Deepdale** 4 miles/1850ft
  via Great Wold,
  Whernside Tarns
- **White Shaw Moss**
  1½ miles/950ft
  via Cable Rake Moss

WALK 9   *6¼ miles/1450ft from Kingsdale*

GRAGARETH   *2057ft/627m*

Start from hilltop lay-by almost 1½ miles north of Thornton-in-Lonsdale on Dent road before it descends into Kingsdale
SD 691756; LA6 3PB   ***Map: OL2***

Corrupted from its older name of Greygarth, this is the only Lancashire mountain to be found in the Dales. It is a continuation of the long ridge running south from its higher neighbour Great Coum, and forms a huge barrier between the valleys of Leck Beck and Kingsdale. The latter is an absolutely classic glaciated valley, with long limestone scars seaming Gragareth's lower flanks. Caves and potholes punctuate its slopes, most notably in the vicinity of the Turbary Road and on Leck Fell. Kingsdale also features the easily accessed Yordas Cave, a Victorian showcave named from a legendary Norse giant. The Three Men of Gragareth are an iconic trio of cairns on a rash of boulders on the western flank overlooking isolated Leck Fell House: the lonely valley of Ease Gill features the underworld of Ease Gill Caverns (see page 64).   ***From Kingsdale***

GRAGARETH • WALK 9

Pass through the gate at the lay-by and head away on a grassy track, going left of a small installation then winding up to a brow with a wall to your left. Whernside and Ingleborough are already seen back across Kingsdale. The way runs on through a gate in a sturdy wall, with fine limestone scenery through which you will return just up to your right. Remain on the main track which crosses a hollow to rise gently to a saddle ahead. The grassy way curves right into a limestone hollow, winding quickly up to the edge of an empty plateau with Gragareth dominant ahead. The splendid path bears left across this to reach a firmer wallside track. This is the Turbary Road, of which more later.

Go left here, the wall soon turning off and the rougher track dropping away. With grass verges it swings down to the right, and down to a gate where it becomes enclosed. Just 50 yards further down, a stile on the right sends an initially stone-flagged path across reedy pasture. As the stones end it rises gently away, its objective of a wall on the brow marked by white-painted blobs. However, an interesting detour leaves the path early on: after a large shakehole a thin trod rises right, passing a more distinctive hole containing a fenced shaft. The way quickly rises to the unmistakable setting of Marble Steps Pot in its shroud of beech trees. This impressive pothole has a sizeable entrance and drops as far as some 400 feet below ground.

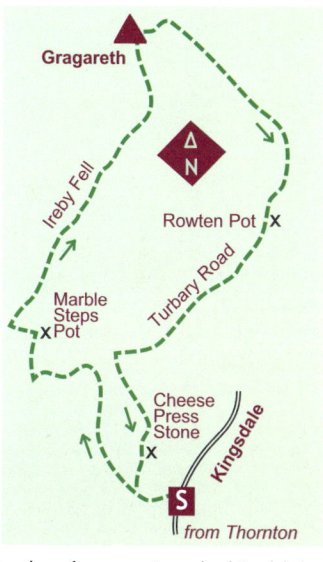

Resume by contouring across to the aforementioned white blobs at a stile in the boundary wall. While a level path heads across Ireby Fell, instead turn right with the wall on a gently rising faint trod. Soon reaching a hollow, drop into it near two tiny pools to a quad track. This rises with a parallel wall opposite, remaining unchanged on a long, gentle ascent. Shortly after a briefly steeper section, the track bears right back to your earlier wall to the top of this tapering enclosure. Just short of the end, a gate on the right sends a path rising 100 yards to a ladder-stile back over the wall. This puts you onto Gragareth's summit area, and a faint trod heads away with the sturdy wall. Soon reaching

WALK 9 • GRAGARETH

a bend, a clear path diverges steadily away for a very gentle rise to reveal and then soon reach the Ordnance Survey column. Gragareth's position on the edge of the Dales renders this an extensive viewpoint. Far-reaching views look out to Pendle Hill, Bowland, Morecambe Bay, the Lune Valley, the limestone lower heights of Hutton Roof Crags and Whitbarrow, and the Lakeland Fells. The Dales peaks are dominated by Gragareth's neighbours Middleton Fell, the Howgill Fells, Great Coum and Whernside, with nearby Ingleborough inevitably magnificent.

Leave by a clear path north-east past several pools to rejoin the wall at a stile just before a fence joins it. Across, head away with a wall on your right, a thin path rapidly reaching the crest of a surprisingly steep but short stage of the descent. The wallside path winds down by scattered boulders and scree, easing to descend intermittently moistly all the way to a wall corner. Through the gate/stile a largely grassy track slants down to level out, swinging right to a gate onto the Turbary Road. Its grassy course will remain underfoot for a mile and a half. The next gate reveals the first of its caves, the unmissable Rowten Pot.

Rowten Pot is the pride of Gragareth's potholes, a visual feast that reveals itself suddenly and dramatically. Bedecked in vegetation, this irregular gaping chasm drops some 350 feet into the bowels of the earth. Adjacent is a less obvious, more sinister hole. Across the path is the collapsed roof of Rowten Cave: 100 yards up the moor is the entrance, with the dry hole next to it offering a short adventure.

GRAGARETH • WALK 9

The Three Men of Gragareth, looking towards Middleton Fell

Beyond it the way runs on through intervening gates, for the most part rising ever slightly. Ultimately you reach a gate with, for the first time, a wall on your right just short of the track's high point. A minute further is the point where you joined the road, but the last stretch brings added interest by leaving the track immediately after this gate,

The **Turbary Road** is a splendid walkers' way along a limestone shelf. Turbary is the right of commoners to dig peat for fuel, and the track was made for the passage of carts to the Turbary Pasture. Today this splendid walkers' way is perfectly laid out as a springboard for inspection of a range of caves and potholes.

WALK 9 • GRAGARETH

On Gragareth's western flank the limestone underworld of **Ease Gill Caverns** falls within Britain's most extensive complex of underground passages, the Three Counties System. Overlooked by the caving base of Bullpot Farm, the stream of Ease Gill features such celebrated names as Lancaster Hole, County Pot and Cow Pot, with intriguingly named Wretched Rabbit and Bull Pot of the Witches in very close attendance. Downstream, the valley transforms into the contrastingly lush surrounds of Leck Beck.

GRAGARETH • WALK 9

The Cheese Press Stone, looking to Ingleborough

on a clear path left. It crosses a featureless plateau with a wall just to your left to arrive at a limestone pavement stretching away to your right. During this final stage, Ingleborough is seen at its finest. Here the main path bears right, dropping very gently to aim for the distinctive Cheese Press Stone, a huge limestone block. Though briefly lost from sight, remain on the path heading that way: ignoring other branches bearing left, you will soon arrive. Perched on limestone, it hides a smaller companion in this grand setting.

Just yards beyond it, a little path doubles back left down a short slant to a contouring path just below. Amid fine limestone scenery go right above a shattered pavement, rising just feet to a modest brow. It then winds down to the left and departs the limestone, dropping across the moor to rejoin the outward route at the walk's second gate.

Alternative ascents
- **Leck Fell** 1 mile/700ft
  via Three Men of Gragareth
- **Ireby** 3½ miles/1650ft
  via Ireby Fell
- **Masongill** 3 miles/1500ft
  via Ireby Fell
- **Kingsdale Head**
  1½ miles/1100ft
  via Yordas Cave

WALK 10   *7½ miles/1850ft from Dent*

GREAT COUM   *2254ft/687m*

Start from the village centre, car park
SD 704870; LA10 5QL   Map: OL2

    Great Coum occupies a prominent location above Dent village on the south side of Dentdale, with the side valley of Deepdale beneath its eastern flank. It sends ridges south via its subsidiary top of Green Hill (2060ft/628m) to link with Gragareth, and south-west over Crag Hill to drop to the caving base of Bullpot Farm, while Ease Gill penetrates from the same area deep into the fell's south-western flank. The unfrequented western slopes fall to lonely Barbondale. The fell takes its name from a vast grassy hollow (an uncommon Dales feature) scooped out of the slope just east of its summit. Contouring around its northern flank is the Occupation Road, a walled lane linking the roads from Dent to Ingleton and Barbon: this old packhorse way and service road for the enclosures provides some sweeping views over Dentdale.

From Deepdale

GREAT COUM • WALK 10

From the car park head along the cobbled street in the village centre, keeping left at the George & Dragon to drop to Church Bridge. Don't cross the bridge but take a path on the right heading upstream by the River Dee, immediately deflected from it by Keld Beck. Follow this just as far as a bridge on it, across which advance to a kissing-gate just ahead, then running with a wall as it guides the path back to the river. Simply head upstream on a largely enclosed path that faithfully shadows the enchanting Dee. High to your right are the Megger Stones fronting Great Coum. Keep straight on the riverbank at a junction with a bridleway after an adjacent ford and stepping-stones. Ahead, mighty Whernside encloses Deepdale. Two minutes beyond the ford, a major confluence with Deepdale Beck makes a lovely spot. Great Coum's summit dome is now visible, set well back from the Megger Stones. Deepdale Beck is now your companion to Mill Bridge, where you emerge onto a road.

Go left just a few strides but don't cross the bridge, instead take a stile on the right sending a path upstream. Leave this almost at once on a lesser path slanting right to double back up above the low wooded bank. Entering the first of two meadows, your route up them may well be pathless: if there's a path going left, trace it 50 yards then slant right to meet a level cross-path. Across, simply ascend to a hedge-stile above, and resume similarly to an outer wall corner to run with the wall the short way to a corner stile onto narrow Deepdale Lane. A short way to the left at Peacock Hill Farm, turn right up a short-lived concrete drive at High Nun House, continuing as a rough lane encased in greenery. This is Nun House Outrake, interminably stony for some time until emerging from trees and rising to a gate, where it becomes wider and grassier. This long pull ends at a T-junction with the similarly enclosed Occupation Road.

Turn left on this track's walled course, rising only ever steadily for rather longer than half a mile until a rusty gate on the right beneath the distinct scar of Binks. A grassy track curves up the rushy pasture, with Ingleborough appearing majestically to the left. This abandoned access

67

WALK 10 • GREAT COUM

road leads to Binks Quarry immediately behind the scar's right edge. Amid substantial blocks of Dent Marble (a dark form of limestone) the track ends, with the vast hollow of Great Combe above. Maintain your direction on a continuing sheeptrod up the near edge of the immense rushy hollow, and when it turns off simply continue up the spur. A steeper section past a rash of stones leads invitingly up the edge to gain the skyline. Bear left to join a path with a wall rising very gently past a wall junction, levelling out to run the short way to a stile in a wall corner on the flat top of your fell.

The highest point is difficult to define: it stands just 50 yards to the right, this side of the wall, and 20 yards out from the wall heading away. A scrappy group of stones five yards out from the wall is not actually it, though in truth it's not really that important: at the end of the day you are on the felltop! More regularly taken as the summit (even though it isn't) is a decent cairn along a path curving away from the ridge-wall beyond crossing the stile: this sits atop a distinct little

The lush valley of **Dentdale** spends several delectable miles along the base of Great Coum, with the sparkling River Dee shadowed throughout its length by the Dales Way path. Dent village is an unhurried backwater with cobbled streets and a couple of pubs. A Shap granite drinking fountain celebrates Dent man Adam Sedgwick who spent over 50 years as Professor of Geology at Cambridge, and did much research into the fascinating geology of his own backyard.

GREAT COUM • WALK 10

hollow, and on the crest of a distinct little brow. Great Coum's position in the western Dales renders it a splendid viewpoint, with the array of Lakeland Fells being magnificent. The much nearer Howgill Fells alone are worth the effort, while the contrasting landscapes of Morecambe Bay and the Three Peaks also feature well.

From the wall-corner stile a good path runs north along the left side of the wall, dropping gently then briefly steeply to a wall junction at Crag End. All of this stage enjoys glorious Dentdale views. Across the stile resume on a faint way, still with the wall and on good terrain. An intermittent quad track helps you along this gentle decline, passing circular shakeholes and eventually terminating at an outer wall corner. While the wall turns off, continue along the rapidly fading quad track straight ahead, becoming a clear little path descending very gently through otherwise poor terrain. It ultimately fades as the Megger Stones appear just ahead.

Advance to this scattering of boulders dominated by a plethora of substantial cairns. This splendid location includes Dent church in view directly below. From the right-hand end a sheep trod contours right to some lesser rashes of stones, then curves along to very quickly reach the site of Whaley's Quarry. A grassy rake slants down towards the wall, fading as it drops left and across a minor reedy tract to a small

A frozen pool on the summit of Great Coum

WALK 10 • GREAT COUM

Dentdale from the Megger Stones

corner gate back onto the Occupation Road. Turn left for a foolproof return, only very gradually losing height and incorporating some good grassy sections: this is an awesome promenade with much of Dentdale outspread. Ultimately arriving at another T-junction, turn right down through a gate to descend Flintergill Outrake.

Stone pillar on The Crag, beneath Great Coum's summit

GREAT COUM • WALK 10

The County Stone on the ridge leading to Gragareth from Great Coum, where the real Yorkshire, Lancashire and Westmorland meet

Initially grassy and open, you soon reach a gate into the gill's wooded confines. A stile on the left accesses a toposcope detailing the magnificent view. The descent is now entirely wooded as Flinter Gill tumbles over rock ledges in a deep ravine. Part way down, a gate on the left just after a restored limekiln gives access to High Ground barn with its display of farming implements. Becoming stony, the track drops to the village edge. The way briefly narrows to re-enter Dent, then as a narrow lane drops past a small green and the school to the centre.

Alternative ascents
- **Dent** 3¼ miles/1800ft
  via Flinter Gill, Megger Stones
- **White Shaw Moss** 2½ miles/750ft
  via County Stone, Gatty Pike
- **Keldishaw** 2¾ miles/1350ft
  *via Occupation Road,
  Towns Fell, Crag End*
- **Bullpot** 3 miles/1300ft
  via Crag Hill
- **Bullpot** 4 miles/1450ft
  via Ease Gill, County Stone

WALK 11   *8 miles/2200ft from Barbon*

MIDDLETON FELL   `2000ft/610m`

Start from the village centre, roadside parking
SD 628825; LA6 2LJ   *Map: OL2*

    Named from a scattered Lune Valley hamlet, the sprawling mass of Middleton Fell is very much a detached parcel of upland. Prior to 2016 it was largely outwith the national park as a result of its allegiance to old Westmorland. Resembling the Howgill Fells in character, its occasional slaty outcrops stand best comparison with Black Combe in the southern Lake District. Its slatiness is matched by its deeply incised western gills, its heather flanks and its isolation: Middleton Fell has no appreciable links to other ground. Its finest feature is the craggy scoop of Combe Scar hovering above Gawthrop in Dentdale, while very steep slopes also fall east into Barbondale. The summit is known as Calf Top. Listed at a tantalising 1999ft on trusty old One-Inch maps, a 2016 survey elevated it to the 2000ft mark with a millimetre or two to spare. Current maps show it as 610m, rounded up from 609.6m.   ***From Keldishaw***

MIDDLETON FELL • WALK 11

From the war memorial leave the village by the road past the Barbon Inn and the church, then turn left along the drive into Barbon Park. Across the bridge on Barbon Beck the drive swings right to start to climb towards Barbon Manor hidden in the trees. But immediately meeting a path crossroads, go sharp left across the pasture to pass right of a wood. From a gate at the end keep on to the house at Eskholme. Though the path strictly enters the grounds to immediately re-emerge on the right, instead simply turn sharp right to ascend to a gate at the top. Entering open country, this is the last one until you pass back through to finish. The ascent begins in earnest, first objective being the unseen cairn on Eskholme Pike set back above Devil's Crag directly above. Take the grassy quad track slanting left, and when it soon runs left, take a continuing slighter one ahead, enjoying a super slant up to beneath low crags. It swings right here as a thinner way, soon rising more directly past some scattered rocks to almost fade on a shelf. From here bear briefly right to cross to the big cairn on Eskholme Pike's rocky plinth. This moment merits a halt to survey the superb panorama over the Lune Valley – and also far beyond.

Behind the cairn a good path sets an obvious course along the crest of the broad ridge, widening into a quad track. Visible ahead is the cairn on Castle Knott, some way off and still some way short of the main summit. The slope eases further before a mildly stiffer pull, the path occasionally thinning slightly before gaining a tidy cairn. The bulk of Great Coum now looms ahead across unseen Barbondale. Passing above a clutch of tiny pools the path swings left beneath grassy knolls, and up ahead the top of Castle Knott beckons. A level section precedes the short pull, noting an old sheepfold on a rash of stones across to the left. Gaining Castle Knott's cairn at 1765ft/538m, a surprise awaits in the form of a sizeable depression interrupting the march to the finally visible summit. The environs of Castle Knott offer dramatic views over Barbondale to Baugh Fell, Widdale Fell and Great Coum. A briefly

WALK 11 • MIDDLETON FELL

steeper drop to the saddle precedes a short moist section, then a peaty section amid heather precedes a grand pull on a broad path to gain the summit ridge. An old wall/fence corner is reached before the summit, to guide a short, marginally rising stroll along to the Ordnance Survey column. The highest point is apparently a few strides to the south-east.

Eskholme Pike

The summit grants extensive views over the north-west counties: over the fence is a contrasting close-up down its sheer east flank. To the west are Morecambe Bay and a big Lakeland skyline, northwards are the Howgill Fells, while closer still is Dentdale in its surround of fells. Whilst the obvious option is the pleasurable retracing of steps, consider an excellent circular route. A trod heads west directly away from the summit over barely declining ground, quickly joining a quad track coming in from the right. This will remain your route all the way down to the intake wall. It runs past a small pool, over a slight rise and on to reveal the 7ft stone pillar of Sammy's Pike just to the left.

The track now commences a splendid descent with big Lune Valley views, later entering heather and maintaining a generally straight line down to a more defined if modest 'edge'. The second half of the descent starts here, dropping a little more steeply to briefly fade: it can be picked up by dropping right to revive in a flatter, grassy area. Here it runs briefly level to the right, leaving heather and quickly doubling back left. Dropping a little faintly at the onset of bracken, it quickly swings left again, crossing a streamlet to commence a superb grassy slant down the bracken-clad fellside. It leads all the way to the base of the fell, emerging from bracken two minutes above the intake wall.

MIDDLETON FELL • WALK 11

The return track descending towards the Lune Valley

Within 100 yards of the wall drop left to the foot of the tree-lined ravine of Millhouse Gill, beneath a nice waterfall. Cross and rise briefly with the intake wall, quickly escaping encroaching bracken either by remaining with the wall or directly up to then contour back to the wall. A decent sheeptrod eases you on a level course above the wall through intermittent bracken. As the wall drops away, bear left over a streamlet, slanting up to cross a larger streamlet to gain a wall corner up ahead. Continue above this, again largely on a sheeptrod. With Eskholme Pike appearing ahead, retain the contouring trod past a few rocks and on to more bracken. A green path drops down into the bracken, but at an early wall corner, bear off left to contour across, soon beneath the limit of the bracken. Ignoring the lower intake wall, cross towards a wall corner ahead. Crossing Ashdale Gill just before it, don't join the wall but make use of an excellent, slightly higher trod enjoying a sustained contour on better terrain. Ultimately this meets the outward quad track just above the gate. Drop down to it to conclude as you began.

Alternative ascents

- **Middleton Head**
  4¾ miles/1750ft
  via Fellside, Long Bank, Barkin Top
- **Holme Fell** 5 miles/1750ft
  via Long Bank, Barkin Top
- **Barbondale** 2 miles/1600ft
  via Castle Knott

WALK 12 — 6 miles/1500ft from Cowgill

WIDDALE FELL — 2205ft/672m

Start from Stone House Bridge a mile south, parking on west side
SD 770859; LA10 5RL   *Map: OL2*

Widdale Fell forms a large upland wedge between delectable Dentdale to the west and the bleak valley of Widdale to the east. Its broad, high-level ridge running north-east towards Wensleydale is soaked in peat groughs and is seldom frequented: at its shapelier northern limit on Sandy Hill the ground falls quite steeply to hidden Mossdale. The ridge supports Widdale Great Tarn and Widdale Little Tarn. The fell shows its steeper, more defined side to the valley that named it, though Widdale itself is known only for the road linking Ribblehead to Hawes. The fell's western flank hosts two fine rail viaducts as well as Dent Station. The Galloway Gate track contours around this western flank at a higher level than the railway, a route used by Scottish drovers bringing cattle to markets further south. The summit name of Great Knoutberry Hill is commonly but mistakenly used for the entire fell.   *From Widdale*

WIDDALE FELL • WALK 12

The hamlet of Stone House is the site of a 19th century marble works: the celebrated Dent Marble is actually a dark limestone, seen very effectively in the viaduct above. The River Dee flows delightfully over limestone slabs under the narrow stone-arched bridge, while looming behind is the majestic Arten Gill Viaduct. From the bridge leave the viaduct side of the valley road on a short road rising past Stone House Farm and a tiny handful of dwellings. When it swings down to Artengill Beck take a gate in front and a walled track climbs steeply towards the viaduct. The going eases as you pass under it and look back to appraise the sprawl of Whernside across the dalehead.

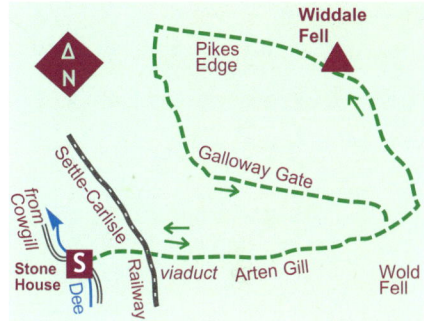

Through a gate behind, the track settles down to a prolonged, gentler ascent up the side of Arten Gill. Great Coum now features in the view back down the valley, soon joined by Middleton Fell: your route is an old trail from the western Dales over to market at Hawes. The going only eases at a track crossroads in front of Arten Gill Moss Gate. The left branch is to be your return, so for now take the gate in front for a very short, gentle rise alongside a wall to the very brow of the track. At 1725ft/526m this marks the start of its descent into Widdale. Ahead is the bulk of Dodd Fell, with Widdale Fell's flat underling Wold Fell down to your right.

From a stile in the wall corner commence a steady ascent on a good grassy path close to the wall that will lead to the summit. Shapely Pen-y-ghent appears almost at once, soon followed by Ingleborough. A few gritstone rocks are passed, and the going eases further for the upper half as the wall swings left to run to the summit. An Ordnance Survey column stands in a small pool at a junction with fences: in the acute angle over the wall is a sturdy structure with seating. This typical Pennine felltop boasts an outstanding view, greatest features being the prospect of Dentdale running away to the west, and the triple profiles of the Three Peaks. Though Ingleborough and Pen-y-ghent regularly express themselves favourably, they rarely have the company of a shapely Whernside. Widdale Little Tarn can be glimpsed, while the sudden revelation northwards sees the dramatic profile of Wild Boar Fell leading to High Seat above Mallerstang Edge.

WALK 12 • WIDDALE FELL

Widdale Great Tarn

Leave by resuming your direction, now with a fence heading west back towards Dentdale. Initially damp, this flatter upper section reveals a glimpse of the sizeable Widdale Great Tarn over to the right. The terrain improves as you commence the descent proper, the path enjoying a glorious steady descent with the verdant floor of Dentdale backed by Great Coum and Middleton Fell. The well-defined Pikes Edge is a good place to pause, with scattered rocks and a shapely cairn along the modest escarpment: Dent station is also revealed below. From here it is but minutes further down the fenceside to gates and a stile at sheep pens onto the inviting track known as Galloway Gate.

The **Settle-Carlisle Railway** runs for several miles along Widdale Fell's western flank high above Dentdale, and boasts two mighty viaducts constructed over their deeply-carved gills in 1875. Dent Head Viaduct's ten limestone arches reach 100ft in height, with Arten Gill Viaduct's eleven Dent marble arches taller still. Also here, incredibly some four miles from its village, is Dent Station, the highest mainline station in England at 1145ft/350m.

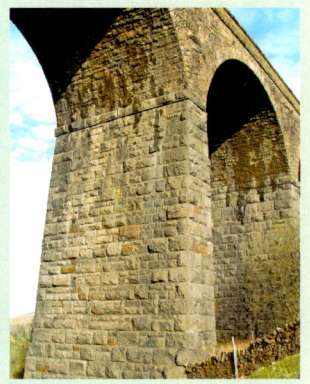

WIDDALE FELL • WALK 12

Dentdale from Pikes Edge, with a train leaving Dent Station

Turn left through a gate to commence a memorable stroll along the grassy carpet of this wallside track. Though it largely contours the fell's western flank, you will quickly note that it does also gain a little height as you progress. Further on, the track becomes enclosed by walls, and swings left to reveal the cleft of Arten Gill below, and then the viaduct. Your way rises very comfortably to its highest point at 1784ft/543m, before dropping to a gate back onto the bridleway cross-roads at Arten Gill Moss Gate. Turn right to retrace the opening stage all the way back under the viaduct.

Alternative ascents
- **Dent Station**
  2¼ miles/1100ft
  via Coal Road, Galloway Gate, Pikes Edge
- **Widdale Foot**
  3¼ miles/1300ft
  via Arten Gill Gate
- **Newby Head Gate**
  2¾ miles/1000ft
  via Wold Fell, Arten Gill Gate

WALK 13 *10 miles/1650ft from Hawes*

DODD FELL *2192ft/668m*

***Start from the town centre, car parks
SD 875898; DL8 3NT   Map: OL2***

Occupying a central position in the heart of the Dales, Dodd Fell is one of its more unassuming hills. Its pivotal location is confirmed by the fact that the major rivers of Ure, Wharfe and Ribble all gather water from its slopes: indeed the source of the latter is found at Gavel Gap to the south-west. The fell's principal feature is a slender, high-level ridge running north to Ten End, before descending towards Gayle and Hawes in Wensleydale. A high-altitude connection, much used by minor roads, links it by way of Fleet Moss to Wether Fell. The eastern flanks fall to Sleddale, while the steep western slopes fall to lonely Snaizeholme, an offshoot of Widdale: the spur of Snaizeholme Fell curves around to enclose it. Southern slopes fall to Oughtershaw Beck, a co-founder of the Wharfe. The Romans' Cam High Road from Ingleton to Bainbridge traverses these slopes just 330ft/100m lower than the summit - known as Dodd Fell Hill.   ***From above Gayle***

DODD FELL • WALK 13

This route follows Pennine Way signs almost all the way to the top. Leave past WCs alongside a car park on the main street almost opposite the Board Inn. A path rises into a higher car park, then from a stile in the top wall bears right across a field to the Gayle road. Turn left past Wensleydale Creamery into the characterful heart of Gayle. Reaching an arched bridge over tumbling Gayle Beck, don't cross but take a short, setted way on the right. Continue along a lane to an old kissing-gate up steps after the last house on the left. Already with big views back over Hawes and across the valley, climb half-right past a wall corner to a stile ahead. Wether Fell rises to the left, with Dodd Fell straight ahead. Take the path directly away to a stile ahead, followed by another, then along to one onto the access road of Gaudy Lane. Just a few strides right, turn left up the drive towards Gaudy House.

Before the entrance gate take one on the left, and the grassy path of West Cam Road makes a sustained rise up a rough pasture close by the wall. From a top corner gate, it resumes more gently with a wall on the left, rising to a gate. The path runs on past a solid cairn around to a gate to resume. Rising onto a bigger shelf, the way soon slants right away from the wall. Passing left of a reedy area beneath a steeper slope, the path rises gently to a gate in a cross-wall. With the valley of Snaizeholme below, the path runs a level course along the crest of Ten End with the vestige of a wall.

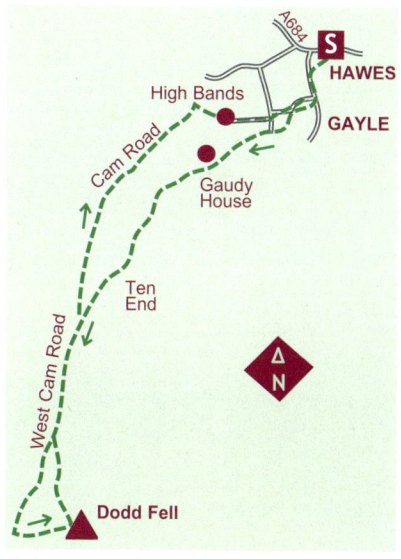

When a branch rises left, keep straight on, crossing the old wall and on past a line of shakeholes, with Ingleborough appearing ahead. Soon joining the firm track of West Cam Road, bear left on its rapidly improving course. So begins a sustained contour of a mile and a half, with accompanying walls coming and going. After a lengthy open stage, you are rejoined by a wall from the right to run along the base of the steeper upper slopes. A stonier spell above a marked drop to

WALK 13 • DODD FELL

Looking south to Pen-y-ghent from Dodd Fell

Snaizeholme precedes arrival beneath a distinctive cairn up to the left. This hovers above a dry, stony ravine, with limestone shakeholes at its foot. Here, by a solitary boulder, finally break off and ascend the ravine's left side with a faint path appearing. Quickly gaining the brow, the trod rises imperceptibly left to the uppermost plateau, and shapely Pen-y-ghent comes into view over to the right. As the Ordnance Survey column appears, negotiate a wet corner and make a moist beeline for it, where it perches fortuitously on a dry platform.

Of particular note in the view are the valleys of Langstrothdale in Upper Wharfedale and the great trough of Wensleydale. An extensive panorama features almost every fell in this book, along with the Bowland moors, Lakeland Fells and North Pennines. While the easiest departure retraces steps, for a variation, head north-west across a brief

Within Dodd Fell's western horseshoe, the secretive valley of **Snaizeholme** has become a stronghold for one of our most treasured and endangered wild mammals. The red squirrel is an iconic character usurped by the larger grey, introduced from America. An enterprising landowner has established a reserve in the pinewoods, with a walking trail and viewing area. On a grander scale, 2023 saw the Woodland Trust commence planting some 100,000 trees around this tired valley in a hugely exciting project for nature and wildlife.

DODD FELL • WALK 13

Looking west across Snaizeholme from Dodd Fell

peaty section. A trod points towards some minor knolls, continuing less moistly to look down on a peaty shelf. As the trod fades, simply slant down pleasant slopes, possibly making for an appreciable rash of boulders. From here a trod drops gently on to merge back onto the West Cam Road by two large shakeholes. Return to the point you joined it, then consider two options: in all honesty it's nicer to return by your ascent route, but a variant return offers a change of scene and is easier in poor weather, so for what it's worth here it is. The old road is quite rough underfoot, and frankly tedious. It drops past a plantation, through a lengthy open area, then down as a walled lane to drop to a junction. Turn sharp right on Bands Lane, dropping to a road-end at High Bands. Either go briefly right to rejoin the outward route, or briefly left to another junction and then right to re-enter Gayle.

Alternative ascents
- **Newby Head** 4 miles/950ft via Jam Sike, Gavel Gap, Cold Keld Gate, Kidhow Gate
- **Gearstones** 5 miles/1250ft via Gayle Beck, Cam High Road, Cam End, Cold Keld Gate, Kidhow Gate
- **Fleet Moss** 1½ miles/350ft via North Gate

WALK 14

8½ miles/1550ft from Hawes

WETHER FELL

2014ft/614m

*Start from the town centre, car parks
SD 875898; DL8 3NT   Map: OL30*

By Dales standards this is a compact hill in an easily accessed central location. Overlooking both Hawes and Semerwater, it offers a range of practical ascent lines. A classic Roman road runs within two minutes of its summit, and the proximity of the highest road in the Dales makes for the easiest mountain ascent in the area. Its name comes from the term for a male sheep relieved of reproductive ability, and the summit is known as Drumaldrace. Wether Fell is bounded by deep valleys to all but south, with high-level links to Dodd Fell, or more distantly to Yockenthwaite Moor via Fleet Moss. Western slopes fall steeply to Sleddale, less so to Raydale to the east. Best feature is the north-easterly spur dropping elegantly all the way to Bainbridge, incorporating the assertive outcrops of Yorburgh and Crag.

From Dodd Fell

WETHER FELL • WALK 14

Leave the market place by a path under an alley just before the church, and across a yard it rises firmly to emerge by the church into a field. It now runs a flagged course through fields above Gayle Beck, with Wether Fell above. Joining the Gayle road, turn left to the bridge. Across, keep right to climb steeply out of the village. An early stile on the left sends a part-flagged path rising away. As the wall turns off, the path bears right up to a stile. Now pathless, cross to a stile ahead, then briefly on a wallside to one onto a track. Go left, fading on reaching a gate with adjacent stile. Continue away across several fields linked by stiles in parallel walls. Entering a larger field, bear slightly right to a corner stile beyond a barn. Rise directly away from this to a stile into the base of a scrubby bank, and a path slants up to a stile at the top.

Entering a steeper pasture, a faint path rises through a line of shakeholes to a gap-stile at the steeper top: continue rising with a small stream to your left. Easing higher up, rise slightly left, joining a path to a gate at the top. A path climbs very steeply away, then swinging left on gentler ground to a gateway in a descending wall. A clear path crosses rough pasture the short way to a corner wall-stile, then runs on to rise gently the same way to a stile/gateway. Just beyond this you join a grassy bridleway, now at equal height with Yorburgh's rear to your left. Turn right, levelling out as the

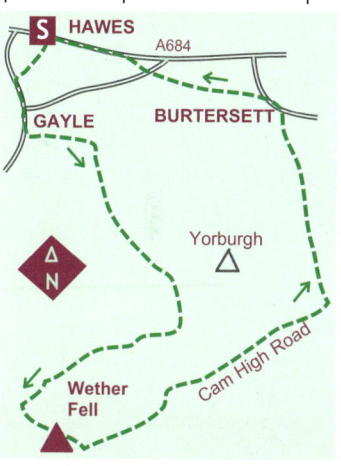

wall quickly turns off, leaving a super path to contour across a shelf to a gate. Through it, remain on the more inviting left-hand sunken track winding up. You are now looking back on Yorburgh, and along to Crag, Addlebrough and Penhill. Ignoring lesser branches, it levels out to run grandly to a gate onto Wether Fell's high moorland.

With the unseen summit set well back defended for now by peat groughs, turn right on a path close by the wall. The summit is quickly revealed some way ahead, but don't abandon this circuitous course: your path is heading ever nearer the top, and temptation to strike out left is best avoided until the slope steepens. Grand level strides lead quickly past an old quarry on Flint Hill. A little further the way makes an insignificant descent with the wall a little lower: through moister

WALK 14 • WETHER FELL

Wether Fell across Semerwater from Addlebrough

terrain you pass further old workings. Just after a small quarried scar, at a slight apex of the wall, the slope ahead starts to drop away again to moister ground, while steeper slopes alongside confirm it's time to leave. Climbing briefly left, things level out at a modest peat castle, revealing the summit cairn two minutes further along a grassy trod. This extensive viewpoint has the Three Peaks, Howgill Fells and Wild Boar Fell all well seen, with the North Pennines beyond Great Shunner Fell.

To begin the return, a path slants two minutes down to the stony track of Cam High Road just to the south. The old road is followed left for some time on its gentle descent: a slight brow reveals Semerwater ahead beneath Addlebrough. Soon enclosed by walls, the point of departure is a mile further, during which you pass twin stiles 75 yards after a bridleway departs right. Reaching another pair of stiles, the left

Cam High Road is the former Roman road from Ribblehead to the fort at Bainbridge. The whole of that section forms an exhilarating high-level march, and Wether Fell is one of two 2000-foot summits it skirts. Though 'improved' further west, several miles of the old highway still remain to provide a gem of a traffic-free walking route.

WETHER FELL • WALK 14

High on Wether Fell

one sends a slender path away, dropping to a stile just past a streamlet. With Yorburgh above, the path enjoys a pleasant, direct descent of this large pasture to a stile left of a wall corner, beyond another streamlet. A few yards over the brow reveal Burtersett, and through an old wall, a steeper drop through reeds improves to slant left down to a stile by a plantation foot. Drop slightly left to successive stiles, then follow the right-hand wall to a stile onto the road in the village of Burtersett.

A few yards left, bear right a short way down the street, then go left at a former chapel into a field. A part-flagged path runs to a stile ahead, then forks. Take the similarly surfaced right branch slanting down the field to a stile, from where a stone-pitched track drops more steeply to a narrowing between walls. Meeting a level path, go left on its straight, flagged course through several stiles. At another fork your flagged way bears right again, on past a barn and through further stiles onto a back road. A few yards left is a stile opposite, and from one just behind it a flagged path resumes across one final field to emerge at the far corner onto the road on the edge of Hawes. Turn left to finish.

Alternative ascents

- **Fleet Moss** 1¹⁄₄ miles/250ft
  via Cam High Road
- **Burtersett** 2¹⁄₄ miles/1100ft
  via Yorburgh bridleway
- **Marsett** 2¹⁄₄ miles/1150ft
  via Cam High Road
- **Countersett** 3¹⁄₄ miles/1100ft
  via Crag, Cam High Road
- **Bainbridge** 4¹⁄₂ miles/1350ft
  via Cam High Road

WALK 15 *10 miles/2200ft from Thwaite*

Lovely Seat 2214ft/675m
Great Shunner Fell 2349ft/716m

Start from the village centre, parking on B6270 by Buttertubs junction to south   SD 892981; DL11 6DR   Map: OL30

Linked by the Buttertubs Pass, these two mountains occupy a massive tract of upland dividing Wensleydale and Swaledale. Great Shunner in particular is a true giant, its broad shoulders conveying Pennine Wayfarers from Hawes to Keld. A high, wide ridge runs west to the High Seat-Lunds Fell group, a particularly remote landscape high above Cotterdale. Lovely Seat's alluring name is insufficient to draw the crowds, and for the blinkered peak-bagger a brief pull from the pass will be their sole experience. Eastwards, mile upon mile of moorland declines towards Grinton Moor, breached only by minor unfenced roads. Mining for lead and coal took place all over these hills, and grouse shooting still does. In recent decades both have seen the destruction of craftsman-built cairns, most notably an entire army of stone men on Great Shunner Fell's Stony Edge, and a fine 10ft beacon beneath Lovely Seat's summit.   *From Sleddale*

LOVELY SEAT & GREAT SHUNNER FELL • WALK 15

From the Buttertubs junction just above the village, advance just 50 yards along the Muker road then go right on an enclosed cart-track. This rapidly swings around to ford Cliff Beck, but a tiny short-cut uses a stone-arched footbridge in a lovely little ravine. The track is rejoined just beyond to ascend a large field, easing to run on through a couple of gates to approach Appletree Thwaite. Continue on above the house to a gate, becoming briefly enclosed as a green way. Across a stream and a field-bottom is a gate onto a walled, grassy way at a tiny barn. Turn up to a T-junction with a firmer track at the top, then briefly left over a stone-arched bridge on a grassy ravine. Just a few strides beyond it, a gate on the right sends a grass track slanting left up to a wall to rise gently and faintly with it. When the wall departs, the track continues up, bearing right to Greenseat Gate by sheep pens at the intake wall above.

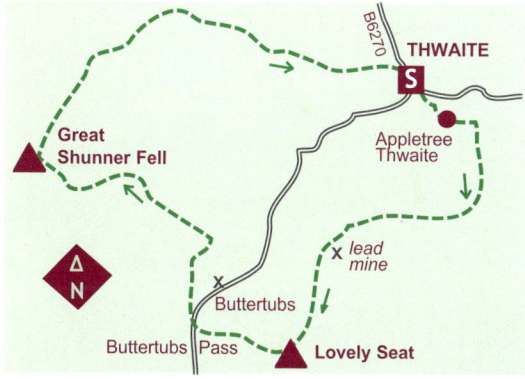

Through the gate turn right across a streamlet for a sustained spell of easy, near-level walking above the intake wall, initially on sheep-trods. Quickly passing beneath an almost hidden impressive limekiln after a low scar, you quickly reach a sheepfold by the wall. Here a trod contours above a dip in the wall before rejoining it for a grassy old track to approach Providence Hush at the Providence Lead Mine. Across the streamlet here, leave the wall and bear left up between extensive spoil heaps, then veer very gently right across the slope. Crossing a long line of shakeholes on a shelf, maintain the gentle crossing to a spread of small boulders, approaching the distinctive ravine of Lover Gill. Curve up the near side to quickly level out, and cross it above a nice little waterfall at its very head. Now bear left for a rougher, moister few minutes, rising gently to ascend a distinct knoll to a collapsed cairn above a modest scattering of rocks. Now bear left

WALK 15 • LOVELY SEAT & GREAT SHUNNER FELL

to gently rise to a cairn with views down Wensleydale. Finish by rising gently right, and after twenty yards the summit appears just 200 yards further. Lovely Seat's highest point is a pleasant grassy dome crowned by a shelter incorporating a seat, with a cairn nearby. The view includes the Three Peaks, and a long line of the North Pennines.

To the west Great Shunner Fell awaits, and a little path runs west for 60 yards, dropping marginally to a fence-stile. Though a thin trod heads away, remain on a clearer path bearing right with the fence. Largely as a quad track it leads nicely down to the road on the crest of the Buttertubs Pass, the flatter final section being moister. Across the cattle-grid commence an entirely foolproof two and a quarter-miles ascent of Great Shunner Fell, with the adjacent fence as an infallible guide. A little path quickly forms to pass an early beacon up to the plateau of Hood Rigg - briefly heading away from the hill as it keeps to the watershed. After a sharp right-angle left through insignificant Grimy Gutter Hags, the path fades for a spell. At a modest bend left a quad track suddenly forms, and this runs on to enjoy a nice rise on grassier terrain slightly away from the fence.

Linking Wensleydale and Swaledale, at 1725ft/526m **Buttertubs Pass** is perhaps the best known of the lofty passes connecting the valleys of the Dales. The Buttertubs themselves are a series of dramatically fluted, deep limestone shafts on the very roadside above the descent to Swaledale. They were supposedly named as farmers bound for Hawes market would lower down their produce to keep it cool. The pass achieved new fame as a classic stage of the 2014 Tour de France.

LOVELY SEAT & GREAT SHUNNER FELL • WALK 15

Merging with the fence on a brow, it swings sharply left on the gentle dome of Little Shunner Fell and through a moister saddle to meet a wall-end. Continue with the fence, across another plateau and a moister section precedes a short pull to the fence-top. With the summit just ahead, the path runs on to quickly meet the stone-flagged course of the Pennine Way at a bridle-gate, with the summit just yards through it. A cross-wall wind shelter is a feature of this exposed top, an addition to the Ordnance Survey column. The fell's altitude ensures massive views of most of the Dales, while a distant Lakeland skyline stretches all the way from the Coniston Fells to Blencathra, including the Scafell group over Wild Boar Fell's plateau.

On Lovely Seat:
Limekiln above Greenseat Gate;
Providence Lead Mine

WALK 15 • LOVELY SEAT & GREAT SHUNNER FELL

Great Shunner Fell from Lovely Seat

Commence the descent by returning to the bridle-gate, simply remaining on the Pennine Way all the way. Much of it has stone flags underfoot, passing several old cairns and a craftsman-built modern one on the knoll of Shunner Fell Rake. A long section down to a saddle precedes a grassy break past a cairn on the brow of Stony Band. The

The **Pennine Way** is England's most famous long-distance path, opened in 1965 to carry walkers along the backbone of England from Derbyshire to the Scottish border. Of its 270 miles, some 55 are spent in the Yorkshire Dales between Gargrave and Tan Hill. Along with Pen-y-ghent, Great Shunner Fell is the only summit it claims.

LOVELY SEAT & GREAT SHUNNER FELL • WALK 15

Meadow under Kisdon near the end of the walk at Thwaite

path runs on then down past a spoil heap from old coal workings before becoming enclosed at a gate. This walled cart-track leads all the way, stonier in its middle, steeper section before improving again on levelling out for a dead-straight finish. A more pleasing conclusion leaves the lane not far from the end, where with gates on both sides just after sheep pens on the left, take the right-hand one. A little path drops to a gap-stile just below, then a clearer path drops slightly left almost to Thwaite Beck. Turn left to run just above it through several meadows linked by gap-stiles. Passing a barn the path runs on to a gate at the end, joining a road just two minutes out of the village.

Alternative ascents

Great Shunner Fell
- **Hardraw** 4¾ miles/1600ft
  via Pennine Way
- **Thwaite** 3½ miles/1500ft
  via Pennine Way
- **Buttertubs** 2½ miles/650ft

Lovely Seat
- **Sedbusk** 3½ miles/1300ft
  via High Clint,
  High Millstones
- **Muker** 3½ miles/1550ft
  via Greenseat Gate
- **Buttertubs** ¾ miles/500ft

WALK 16

7¾ miles/1600ft from Keld

ROGAN'S SEAT

2205ft/672m

Start from the village centre, car park
NY 892011; DL11 6DZ   Map: OL30

Stood high above the northern moors of Swaledale, Rogan's Seat is one of Yorkshire's loneliest mountains. Its vast tracts of rolling heather moorland feature much prized grouse-shooting country. To the east the highest ground leads around to its subsidiary top of Water Crag at 2192ft/668m. The featureless higher reaches contrast starkly with the deep folds of Swinner Gill and Gunnerside Gill falling towards the Swale, and Punchard Gill above Arkengarthdale. Extensively worked for lead predominantly during the 19th century, much evidence of this industry still scars these lower slopes. The northern slopes fall gently towards the famous Tan Hill Inn, highest pub in the country: small-scale coal-mining sites dot this area, with some deep shafts surviving. The name derives from an unknown Norse settler from more than 1000 years ago.

From Kisdon

ROGAN'S SEAT • WALK 16

Leave the bottom right corner of the square by a broad, walled path past a barn. Quickly reaching a fork, take the left branch steeply down to a footbridge on the River Swale. Across, a path curves up above the delightful East Gill Force to a junction where the Pennine Way and Coast to Coast Walk meet. Turn right over the stone-arched bridge and a broad track rises away, up through a gate and on above a steep, fenced scree slope high above the Swale Gorge. Beyond an intervening gate the way soon opens out to swing round past a barn beneath Beldi Hill lead mining remains. Quickly reaching a fork, go left, although a second fork just beyond will merge with the first path. With either option, the way rises a little to quickly run on above the substantial remains of Crackpot Hall.

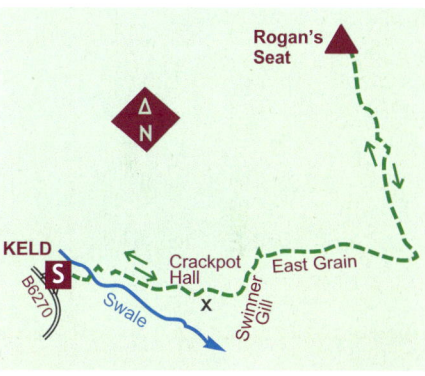

The track briefly climbs beneath some sizeable spoil heaps to run on as a grassy way past a derelict building to soon reach a gate into the rugged confines of Swinner Gill. After a very brief landslipped section just beneath a modest crag, the path slants down across a heathery flank to a stone-arched bridge beneath the ravine of Swinner Gill Kirk: en route note a fine waterfall at the foot of the side valley of East Grain opposite. The path now runs right the short way to the remains of a lead smelting mill. A pleasant climb ensues up the deep enclave of East Grain, noting occasional waterfalls along the way. As the gradient eases, an increasing stretch of stone flags eases progress, passing an old sheepfold to join a stony shooters' track. This rises left before crossing the moortop to a junction on the very brow at 1900ft/580m, just a minute beyond a gate/stile.

Here turn left on the track striking north almost entirely through heather, rising only ever gently with the fence close by to your left. On a peaty shelf you pass a wooden shooters' cabin, and after a kink between deep peat hags, the track resumes its final climb. When the fence finally departs left, the track bears right to quickly level out on the summit area. The cairn stands a good 100 yards to the left on a peaty upthrust, and a thin trod runs out to it from a few rocks just beyond a larger rock cluster.

WALK 16 • ROGAN'S SEAT

Swinner Gill is a colourful ravine amid Upper Swaledale's stunningly beautiful scenery. This small side valley features numerous little waterfalls as it tumbles into the River Swale by way of craggy walls amid lead mining remains. Along with Grassington in Wharfedale, Swaledale was the busiest of lead mining areas, the industry dating back at least to Roman times. It reached a frenzied peak in the late 18th and early 19th centuries, then rapidly collapsed as the best veins were worked out, and replaced by cheaper foreign imports. The smelting mill at the foot of East Grain stands just across the beck from rocky Swinner Gill Kirk, and ruins, levels, shafts and spoil heaps abound.

ROGAN'S SEAT • WALK 16

Rogan's Seat moors from Keld

Coal shaft near Tan Hill

The summit is suitably bleak, being extensively flat, peaty and largely featureless. The peat castle on which the previous cairn stood, pictured below, has largely succumbed to Yorkshire weather. While the view takes in much of the northern Dales, it will be best remembered, on a clear day, for the big prospect west to Lakeland, and north across Stainmore to the rolling North Pennines. As you are returning to Keld the same way, the route description ends here!

Alternative ascents
- **Gunnerside**
  4¼ miles/1500ft
  *via Jingle Pot Edge,
  Lownathwaite*
- **Muker**
  5 miles/1700ft
  *via Arn Gill,
  Swinner Gill*

WALK 17 *6 miles/1050ft from Lamps Moss*

NINE STANDARDS RIGG *2172ft/662m*

Start from Hollow Mill Cross on B6270 summit, parking area on county boundary   NY 811040; CA17 4JR   Map: OL19

Nine Standards Rigg is the last bastion of the Dales, even though the 2016 National Park extension left it as the only summit outside its boundary. It remains within a quarter-mile, and is part of the North Pennines National Landscape (previously AONB). Due to this it has seen curious omission from at least one guidebook to the fells of the Dales. It stands proudly on the Pennine watershed, as noted by Wainwright when he brought his Coast to Coast Walk this way: its northern and western streams are bound for the Solway Firth, while southern and eastern waters find their way to the Humber Estuary. A broad, swampy ridge runs south to subsidiary top White Mossy Hill (2149ft/655m), then down to a rare scattering of rocks at Millstones. Northern slopes fall to the River Belah, a tributary of the Eden, while eastern slopes drain via Whitsundale into the Swale. The fell is best known for the beacons from which it is named. *From Lamps Moss*

NINE STANDARDS RIGG • WALK 17

Hollow Mill Cross is a small, neatly inscribed boundary stone on the county boundary. Head west along the road for five minutes, as far as an inviting grassy track bearing off right. Quickly merging with one from the left, advance on, keeping left at an immediate fork for a few minutes further to another fork. This time bear right to a nearby fence-gate, and the slimmer but still clear path heads away through scattered limestone pavement, dropping marginally to another fence-gate. Here you meet the very pronounced division of limestone and gritstone, with the peat of Lamps Moss itself to the right. The path bears left over the divide, and runs left with another fence. When this turns off, the path continues on peatier terrain, soon swinging right to drop gently past a pool to meet a wall encircling the head of Dukerdale.

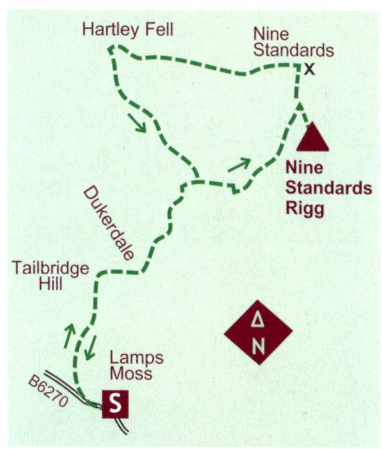

Dropping to cross the often-dry Rigg Beck, the path rises away with the wall to a brow just above. Here the path quickly strikes off right, over mixed ground to cross Rollinson Gill. It then rises briefly to an engineered slant left then up to a shelter-like cairn on a knoll above a rash of stones. Behind it the path continues just 150 yards to a guidepost at a path junction. The now intermittently moist path slants left across gentle slopes, keeping left across a peaty shelf and finishing at a view indicator on the broad summit ridge. At this precise moment the celebrated Nine Standards appear just beyond.

Turn right on a gently rising path the short way to the stone-built Ordnance Survey column on the summit. This is a wonderful place to be: it seems a good half of Northern England is on display from this northernmost summit of the Pennine Dales, and in particular almost all of its mountainous regions. To the south and east are Dales mountains galore, the nearest and most impressive being Wild Boar Fell above Mallerstang, with the rounded Howgill Fells beyond. Further north is the Cross Fell group topping the North Pennines, while the Vale of Eden leads westward to a serrated Lakeland skyline. Whilst you could of course simply retrace steps, it's far more rewarding to enjoy a loop that gives you more interesting time on the hill.

WALK 17 • NINE STANDARDS RIGG

Deemed England's premier long-distance trek, the **Coast to Coast Walk** was devised by Alfred Wainwright in 1973, and each year thousands tramp its 192 miles from St Bees to Robin Hood's Bay. Only on one occasion does it attain higher ground than here on Nine Standards Rigg, where it breaches the watershed of England as it crosses from Kirkby Stephen to Keld.

Resume by returning past the viewpoint to the mighty Standards themselves. Just yards to the left of the principal, central cairn, the route of the Coast to Coast Walk sets off westwards down the hill, an immediately clear path that drops largely pleasantly to a footbridge on a small morass at the beginnings of Faraday Gill. Just beyond is a stone shelter seat, with a neat cairn perched on a knoll opposite. The descent resumes, shadowing the forming ravine of Faraday Gill to approach a wall corner not too far below.

Perched on the northern rim of the broad summit ridge, the **Nine Standards** are celebrated landmarks. Their origin is uncertain, but whether a 'stone army' to deter the Scots long ago or, less excitingly, boundary markers, they are nevertheless a remarkable line of sturdy beacons, and a magnet for Coast-to-Coast walkers crossing the watershed. The fact that the hill is named after them does suggest they've been here for a considerable time.

NINE STANDARDS RIGG • WALK 17

Looking down Swaledale from Millstones, under White Mossy Hill

The path drops to a junction here on Hartley Fell, though you could slant left to cut a small corner and join the broad grassy way at the wall corner. Head away left on a delectable level stroll by the Dukerdale wall. Before long the path slants left for a short pull to a marker post on a knoll. Here keep to the thinner, upper path that slants gently right across a streamlet beneath a ravine. Through this part reedy pasture it quite soon eases to reveal the ascent route's shelter-cairn. Either rise slightly further to the junction guidepost, or short-cut on a sheeptrod to the shelter. Either way all that remains is to retrace steps back to Lamps Moss.

Alternative ascents
- **Hartley**
  4 miles/1700ft
  via Hartley Fell,
  Faraday Gill
- **Birkdale**
  2¼ miles/750ft
  via Millstones,
  White Mossy Hill
- **Raven Seat**
  4 miles/1100ft
  via Whitsundale

WALK 18   *5¾ miles/1600ft from Outhgill*

HIGH SEAT   *2326ft/709m*

Start from The Thrang, ¾-mile south of hamlet on B6259, small parking area   NY 783004; CA17 4JX   Map: OL19

High Seat crowns a high-level ridge running south from the Kirkby Stephen-Swaledale road over Lamps Moss to culminate at Cotter End above Wensleydale. South of the main summit the ridge supports two subsidiary tops, the nearest being Gregory Chapel at 2280ft/695m. Considerably further beyond is Hugh Seat at 2260ft/689m, named from Sir Hugh de Morville, involved in the 12th century assassination of Thomas Becket. Just beneath the summit is the hoary old cairn of Lady's Pillar, recalling 17th century Lady Anne Clifford who owned castles and land hereabouts: the source of the River Eden is just below this point. High Seat is best known for the magnificent rocky escarpment of Mallerstang Edge along its western flank high above the Eden. Contrastingly tame eastern slopes fall to grouse-shooting country in uppermost Swaledale.

From Hazelgill

HIGH SEAT • WALK 18

Virtually opposite the parking area, a stony access road heads away, winding down to bridge the River Eden. From the outset Wild Boar Fell oozes class across the valley. Immediately over, turn downstream with the youthful Eden, with Mallerstang Edge high to the right. Through a couple of fields you reach a gate, where a cart-track runs tight by the river into an extensive barnyard. As the access road swings right at the end, instead go straight ahead to a wall-stile. A path crosses a small pasture to rejoin the river, running pleasantly on through trees to meet an access road. Across the adjacent bridge resume downstream, briefly, and at a wall-end the thin path bears right for the church. A metal kissing-gate accesses St Mary's church, where a tablet over the porch records its restoration by Lady Anne Clifford in 1663. From a gate back onto the road, go very briefly left into the hamlet of Outhgill. Bear right on an access road past an old Methodist chapel and on past a green. A small pinfold at the end features an Andy Goldsworthy sculpture.

The road quickly ends at a gate, where a rougher continuation rises to end at the former school. A gate accesses the open fell, and a thin path rises right with a reedy sunken way to a confluence of Headley's Gill with Outhgill Beck. Go a few yards left with the lesser stream, and the path drops down to cross it. Up the other side it rises as a clear trod up the centre of a broad spur, past a long redundant stile to soon reach a reedy tract. Bear slightly right to resume on the other side of the reeds, the path re-forming to be joined by one from the right. It continues up between distinctive parallel spurs, with the large, walled enclosure of Stone Close just over to the right. A distinctive cairn on the skyline high and directly above is your objective, with the northern reaches of Mallerstang Edge looking aggressively attractive.

The thin path quickly becomes more obvious, slanting right as a very distinct, reedy hollowed way to near the wall. When it swings sharply back left on a less inviting, gentler course, take the thinner trod

WALK 18 • HIGH SEAT

straight ahead to quickly reach a short, level spur running to meet Sloe Brae Gill. Now at the very wall corner, it crosses the stream and rises gently away to quickly arrive above a sidestream's deeper ravine. Don't drop to it, but turn left on a pathless, easy rise above the steeper edge. This soon fades for a gentler, grassy rise as a trod re-forms between reeds. Sloe Brae Gill returns and is traced for some time to approach steeper ground. As the trod fades, cross the streamlet to resume on increasingly steep grass with a large craggy bluff to your right. Higher to the right are the particularly rugged scars of Trough Riggs. The going eases a little and you emerge onto a small reedy shelf, from where a very short rise alongside a rocky groove gains the landmark cairn. Perched on a boulder, this craftsman-built edifice occupies a grand spot overlooking the wonders of Mallerstang.

Swarth Fell and Wild Boar Fell from Mallerstang Edge

Revealed ahead are the gentle uppermost slopes. Behind the rash of stones just above, a trod rises gently to fade just short of the broad summit ridge. While several scrappy cairned knolls might confuse in poor visibility, the equally small summit cairn is neatly identified by a ground level, circular concrete Ordnance Survey trig point alongside. This bare, exposed summit has few equals as a viewpoint. The finest aspect is westwards, where beyond Wild Boar Fell are the Howgill Fells, seen at perhaps just the right distance. The Three Peaks are all very shapely to the south, while the Lakeland skyline stretches all the way from Coniston Old Man to Blencathra.

HIGH SEAT • WALK 18

Under Mallerstang Edge, looking to Swarth Fell

WALK 18 • HIGH SEAT

Turn right (south) on the grassy quad track running along the crest, passing cairned knolls to right then left, the latter revealing the next stage as it drops to the moister saddle of Steddale Mouth. Still largely as a quad track it rises gently to the summit of Gregory Chapel. A large tract of bare ground precedes a scrappy cairn, though feet will be drawn to a substantial cairn on a rash of stones just beyond. With a re-ascent of some 92ft/28m from High Seat, this is the subsidiary top that comes closest to earning 'mountain' status.

Here leave the ridge and bear right on the continuing quad track dropping gently away. Its improving, largely dry course drops steadily to approach the finest section of Mallerstang Edge, here known as Hangingstone Scar. This hugely dramatic moment reveals some vast boulderfields beneath your feet, and the valley floor giving full stature to Wild Boar Fell. The track maintains its gentle descent largely set back from the escarpment, though the initial stage sees a thinner path cling perilously close to the very edge. Quickly arriving at a distinctive pillar, this is the solitary survivor of the iconic Three Men of Mallerstang that long occupied this craggy bluff.

At the base of the fell, on a knoll overlooking the River Eden in Mallerstang, stand the remains of **Pendragon Castle**. Dating from the 12th century, it was owned at times by both Sir Hugh de Morville and Lady Anne Clifford (see page 110). However, it is best known for the legend that a previous structure here was built by Uther Pendragon, father of King Arthur.

HIGH SEAT • WALK 18

Looking north along Mallerstang Edge to Gregory Chapel

The track resumes its gentle decline until, as the edge finally eases, you suddenly have a much thinner path. Above Raven's Nest the path swings off left to a cairned knoll, but it's easier to continue down the pathless final stages, passing above an old land-slipped section to approach a boulderfield. Here turn right down easy slopes, a couple of early reedy passages preceding a short, steady drop to meet Old Road, a continuation of the historic High Way (see Walk 19), at a ford. Turn right for a foolproof conclusion on this firm track's gentle slant, with Mallerstang Edge high above. Towards the end it becomes stonier and swings left to drop to a gate onto the road next to the start point.

Alternative ascents
- **Lamps Moss**
  2 miles/600ft
  via High Pike Hill
- **Pendragon Castle**
  1¾ miles/1500ft
  via Mallerstang Edge
- **Aisgill Moor**
  4¼ miles/1200ft
  via Hell Gill Bridge, Hangingstone Scar
- **Aisgill Moor** 5 miles/1400ft *via Hell Gill Bridge, Hugh Seat*

WALK 19 *5³⁄4 miles/1100ft from Aisgill Moor*

LUNDS FELL *2188ft/667m*

***Start from Aisgill Moor Cottages on B6259, roadside parking,
notably to north   SD 778962; CA17 4JY   Map: OL19***

Taking its name from a scattered hamlet on its south-western slopes above Garsdale Head, this is arguably the dullest of Dales fells. It also suffers the biggest identity crisis, being known in some quarters as Sails, Little Fell or Ure Head. The latter is certainly apt as Wensleydale's great river begins life just a quarter-mile south-west of the summit. Streams also fall north-west from the summit to join Hell Gill Beck, start of the equally mighty River Eden. The fell is a broad, largely featureless ridge, moderately narrowing after crossing an inevitably undistinguished South Top to run south to Cotter End, featuring Cotter End Tarn. Eastern slopes fall into the lonely reaches of West Gill in the secretive valley of Cotterdale. Equally broad, high ridges extend east to Great Shunner Fell and north to High Seat by way of its underling Hugh Seat.   ***From Great Shunner Fell***

LUNDS FELL • WALK 19

Just to the south of the cottages is Aisgill Summit, where at some 1169ft/356m the famous Settle-Carlisle Railway reaches the highest point on a main line in England. Wild Boar Fell rises impressively across the valley. An access track heads away to bridge the railway, then swings left to fork. First take a little path just 50 yards left for a dramatic appraisal of Hellgill Force, where as Hell Gill Beck the infant River Eden makes a vertical drop over a cliff. Your route keeps right, on the main track rising through fields, with Lunds Fell apologetically ahead. Bridging the beck it rises to the house of Hell Gill, where a faint grassy track continues past it up a slender pasture. At a stile/gate at the top you enter a corner of open moorland, on which you will remain until returning to this point. Joining the old road of the High Way, turn right to cross Hell Gill Bridge straddling a very deep ravine.

Remain on the grass track heading away, within just a couple of minutes arriving at a fork. Opt for the grassier left branch, crossing the

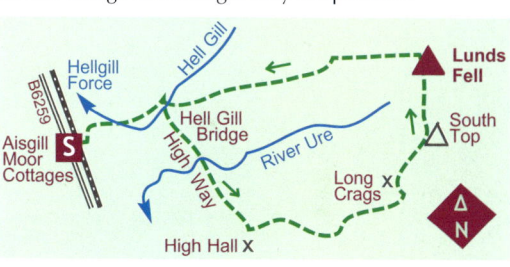

hillside past modest limestone slabs. A wall joins in and the way rises gently to a characterful stream crossing, this being the infant River Ure little more than a mile from its birth. Resuming, the way runs openly again before another wall comes up, this time rising to a wooded ravine at Washer Gill, just around which are the remains of High Hall.

Here leave the High Way and rise left on a grassy quad track opposite the buildings. With Washer Gill down to your left, the way rises above its rim and maintains this parallel course for a considerable time. The gill swings right and then rises left to surmount a distinct brow onto a flat knoll above a scarred section. With an old sheepfold just to your right, this is a good place to perch on the modest rocks just yards to your left. Seen higher up beyond the gill is the bouldery line of Long Crags, with Lund Fell's South Top up behind.

Here you can evade a small, reedy morass by contouring around the rim of the gill to quickly pick up the track. It again shadows the gill, contouring around to a tiny old quarry site on a grassy knoll. The now insignificant gill continues, ultimately crossing it amid reeds to run near a detached group of minor rocks at the start of Long Crags. As the way forks, the left branch runs moistly to and past these to the main

WALK 19 • LUNDS FELL

grouping, which cross to a very distinctive cairn atop them. A neat sheepfold complex sits beneath these particularly jagged rocks. Leave from a scrappy cairn on a flat boulder just short of the quality cairn. It sends a thin path directly away, crossing the quad track and fading as it quickly reaches the final slopes. Continue up, bearing slightly left to reach a cairn in a slight hollow with immediately higher ground just beyond. Joining a ridge-top quad track, go briefly left to gain Lunds Fell's South Top at 2185ft/666m, a few yards west of the track.

Originally deemed the summit, it bears a ground-level trig point alongside a small cairn. A Lakeland view of the Scafells and Great Gable between Swarth Fell and Wild Boar Fell offers one-upmanship on the main summit, which itself is now revealed just a few minutes across a shallow depression. Resume on the track, crossing a minor top: an old cairn further left overlooks Ure Head. A short rise leads pleasantly to the modest cairn on the summit of Lunds Fell. This lonely

The High Way - also known as Lady Anne's Highway - is a famous old track across Lunds Fell's western flank. It is best known as part of the route taken by Lady Anne Clifford on her numerous visits to her Westmorland castles in the 17th century. Now a route for more leisurely travellers, it had for many centuries before formed the major 'highway' running from Hawes to Kirkby Stephen until the arrival of the turnpike road turning off at the Moorcock Inn in 1825. Though the High Way is steeped in history, its one perpetual feature is the prospect of majestic Wild Boar Fell across the valley.

LUNDS FELL • WALK 19

At Long Crags on the upper slopes of the south top

top has an engaging bleakness. Great Shunner Fell looms large to the east, with Wild Boar Fell typically impressive from close range. Much of Lakeland occupies the western skyline, while Cross Fell rises above the Vale of Eden. The Three Peaks all acquit themselves well.

Appraising Hellgill Force in the grip of winter, looking to Lunds Fell

111

WALK 19 • LUNDS FELL

Lunds Fell from a meadow at Garsdale Head

Leave on the continuing quad track dropping invitingly north-west down the broad ridge. Very quickly it swings right, and here you must leave. The least appealing part of the walk sends you left (due west) gently down unkempt, pathless terrain towards a 7ft beacon. This square-set edifice is found to occupy lush green turf on a small rash of

Approaching Lunds Fell from Lunds

LUNDS FELL • WALK 19

Oystercatcher near the infant River Ure

Outer Pike on the descent route, looking north to Hugh Seat

stones on a very minor edge at Outer Pike. It is now a further mile to the High Way: while the pines above Hell Gill Bridge make an obvious target, possibly the best option is to veer further left to parallel Jingling Sike, and in time you might pick up a gently descending quad track. Lower down, this bears right towards the trees at Hell Gill, ultimately dropping by their enclosing fence for the last section down to the High Way at Hell Gill Bridge. Re-cross it to finish as the walk began.

Alternative ascents
- **Aisgill Moor**
  2¼ miles/1050ft
  via Hell Gill Bridge
- **Cotter Riggs**
  4¾ miles/1450ft
  via Cotter End, High Way
- **Garsdale Head**
  4¼ miles/1400ft
  via High Dyke, High Hall

WALK 20

9 miles/1950ft from Aisgill Moor

Swarth Fell
Wild Boar Fell

2234ft/681m
2323ft/708m

Start from Cotegill Bridge on B6259, lay-by half-mile north of Aisgill Moor Cottages SD 774968; CA17 4JY   Map: OL19

With an enticing name and outstanding location, Wild Boar Fell is one of the finest of Pennine hills, the sleek profile of its eastern escarpment readily distinguishable from many Dales fells. All the more surprising that its summit is a plateau so extensive it was used for horseracing. Adjacent Swarth Fell has similar but less dramatic qualities. This upland mass is based on a ridge from Swarth Fell Pike, north over both summits to a classic narrowing at The Nab, then down over Little Fell to the River Eden. A skirt of limestone provides impressive scenery at the pavements of Stennerskeugh and Fell End Clouds, while Low White Kirk ravine at Aisgill boasts a waterfall tumbling into a dark amphitheatre. Swarth Fell Tarn and Sand Tarn are typical upland pools. The fell is named from the last wild boar in England said to have been killed here around 600 years ago by Sir Richard Musgrave, whose Kirkby Stephen tomb when opened in the 19th century revealed a tusk with his remains. *From Aisgill Moor*

SWARTH FELL & WILD BOAR FELL • WALK 20

At an altitude of 1148ft/350m, the start point offers immediately great views of Wild Boar Fell. Head south, away from the rail bridge for half a mile to the county boundary at Aisgill Moor Cottages. From a gate in the fence on the right a very faint quad track rises up the open moor. This steady climb across intermittently moist ground has the wall of Swarth Fell as your objective, not looking too distant given the high altitude start. Looking back across the green floor of Mallerstang, High Seat rises above Mallerstang Edge. Never more than faintly, you rise marginally left, with a wall some 30 yards distant until it turns off. Continue with a defined reedy streamlet to your left. A little higher the way almost levels out to swing steadily left, keeping to the height of land on the broad spur of Stubbing Rigg with Smithy Gill on your right.

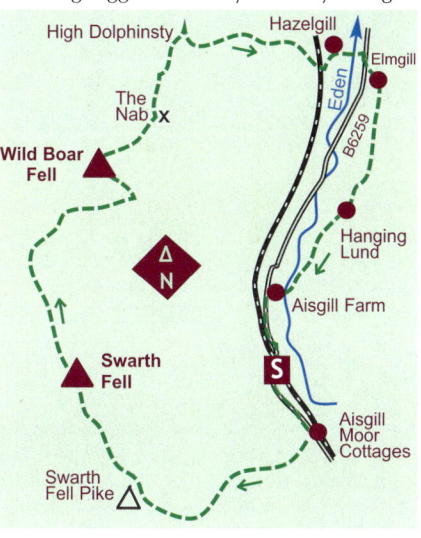

Resuming more directly up alongside the reedy streamlet, you slowly find better ground as the ridge-fence appears not far ahead: beyond it is the bulk of Baugh Fell. The way swings right, rising past a solitary rock to meet a broader quad track shadowing the fence. The view now includes Ingleborough and Whernside to the south, while ahead are the Howgill Fells with Lakeland beyond. Turn right for a steady rise, passing an old cairn to a more substantial one on a brow just ahead.

Now virtually flat, a fork here offers parallel routes to Swarth Fell. Whilst you could opt to remain on the fenceside quad track over the unmarked subsidiary top of Swarth Fell Pike (2136ft/651m), preferably bear right 20 yards to another path junction at a large, isolated boulder. By now Swarth Fell and Wild Boar Fell await ahead. Go left on this excellent, broad path midway between the fence and unseen eastern escarpment for the three-quarters of a mile to Swarth Fell. This runs a splendid, near-level course, through a dip with a pool and scattered rocks for a brief rise to Swarth Fell's summit, marked by a distinctive

WALK 20 • SWARTH FELL & WILD BOAR FELL

Wild Boar Fell and High Seat from Swarth Fell

cairn and a shelter. The cairn stands atop stony outcrops 100 yards out from a wall that has replaced the fence. Inevitably this fine Mallerstang viewpoint has the bulk of Wild Boar Fell as a notable feature.

A clear path bears left past the shelter towards the wall, broadening to drop through the edge of scattered rocks. Joining the wall, it is a pleasant short descent to a partly moist saddle preceding the greater bulk of Wild Boar Fell, with Swarth Fell Tarn to your right. The wall drops off left and a fence returns for a steady pull to a skyline fence corner: just prior to this ignore a more distinct branch curving right. Now on the vast summit plateau, follow the fence on a largely excellent quad track gaining little height. This fades to a trod towards the end, where the fence ends abruptly on sudden arrival at a splendid collection of stone men perched dramatically above a profound drop at High White Scar. This spectacular setting looks down on Wild Boar Fell's great escarpment above tumbled boulderfields, and across the valley to ever-present High Seat above Mallerstang Edge.

Cross the fence-stile to a three-way shelter amid hummocks of old quarry workings. The OS have awarded this the same altitude as the traditional summit a third of a mile across the plateau. Broad green paths set off from the stile and the shelter, rapidly merging at an angled cross-paths where the right branch heads north along the rim. The main branch crosses intermittently marshy ground to rise beyond a tiny pool at the end to gain the Ordnance Survey column within a circular shelter. Unsurprisingly this is an excellent viewpoint, only blank spot

SWARTH FELL & WILD BOAR FELL • WALK 20

High on Wild Boar Fell

being the plateau immediately south, where the ground can appear curiously higher. Various highlights compete for attention, though the Howgill Fells take centre-stage to the west, featuring the outstanding Cautley scene. Also impressive is the scene to the north, with the Westmorland Plateau leading into the Eden Valley backed by the endless ridge of the North Pennines crowned by Cross Fell. A long Lakeland skyline and a fine array of Dales hills also demand attention, with Ingleborough and Whernside forming an elegant twosome.

At High White Scar on Wild Boar Fell's eastern escarpment

WALK 20 • SWARTH FELL & WILD BOAR FELL

Leave by a broad grassy path heading right (north-east). Within 50 yards it forks, the left one running to a distinct cairn. Yours is the right one, which loses only marginal height as it crosses pleasantly to the corner of the plateau at The Nab. Resume by cutting back a few yards on a good path that drops pleasurably above the diminishing edge to a wall corner at High Dolphinsty. Here you meet the Stennerskeugh-Mallerstang track now used by the Pennine Bridleway. Ignoring a path continuing along the ridge to Little Fell, turn right downhill, the first stage being a super grassy slant with The Nab magnificent above.

At the foot of the slant the grassy path drops away left, aided by marker posts past hints of limestone. It then assumes a built course down a wide reedy section, returning to grassiness to drop to a gate in a fence. It resumes to a corner below alongside a littler ravine, where it drops to a gate in front of the stream. Across, it runs out with a wall, continuing on to a sharp zigzag back down to pass underneath the Settle-Carlisle Railway. Drop left through a gate into a field and down towards the former farm at Hazelgill. Don't enter but drop right of the buildings to a track junction, there going left to a gate onto the drive. Go right, bridging the River Eden to join the valley road.

The Nab is one of the most dramatic features on the fells, and at 2303ft/702m its cairn enjoys fantastic views over the Eden landscape. A very brief stroll right on the crest reveals further drama, including a reappearance of the stone men back along the escarpment.

SWARTH FELL & WILD BOAR FELL • WALK 20

Across Mallerstang to High Seat, from an airy stance on Wild Boar Fell

WALK 20 • SWARTH FELL & WILD BOAR FELL

Go right for two minutes to turn left up the short drive to Elmgill, where pass right of the building to a pair of gates set back. From the upper one, a rough track slants up to a gate in an ascending wall. Wild Boar Fell's escarpment now dominates across the valley. For the next half-mile of rough pasture your bridleway isn't visible underfoot: don't follow the rough track up the rough pasture, but go straight ahead through reedy terrain, only a little above the wall below. Above a barn, slant gently up past a marker post. Meeting the wall at an outer corner, resume the slant, actually higher than the bridleway's mapped course. An unmarked bridle-gate in a fence puts you into recently planted woodland some 75 yards higher than the true position. Easiest option in this untidy corner is to descend a fenceside trod for 75 yards, then bear left on a trod along the bridleway's true course.

This traverses beneath scattered trees, rising gently past a gate to reach a bridle-gate out of the enclosure. From the old wall corner in front, advance with the wall to a bridle-gate in an inner corner just ahead. Continue with a wall, the faint way dropping gently to a small gate, then with a wall on the left gently down to a narrowing to resume with a wall on the right. This runs on, soon dropping in sunken fashion to the foot of a stream with lively waterfalls. From a wooden bridge below, rise a few yards to run on outside the grounds of Hanging Lund.

Through a gate to a corner just ahead, drop briefly right outside the grounds to a stile, which don't use. Instead bear left, gently down to a gate. Cross a tiny reedy enclosure past a barn to a gateway into a vast, reed-choked pasture. Initially moist, head away by the wall on

Walkers ascending to The Nab, with the Upper Eden Valley behind

SWARTH FELL & WILD BOAR FELL • WALK 20

Fell End Clouds, looking to the Howgill Fells

your left, rapidly improving to run to a corner stile at the end. Cross to a gateway and then a wall-stile ahead. Advance to cross an access road beneath a house, then bear right to a wall-stile above a short drop to the tree-lined Eden. Advance on with a wall outside its course, through a gateway then a gate just short of a farm bridge on the river. Cross to rise into Aisgill Farm, bearing right to run on to emerge back onto the road. Go left for a gentle half-mile rise to re-cross the railway to finish.

Alternative ascents

Wild Boar Fell
- **Stennerskeugh**
  3¼ miles/1500ft
  via High Dolphinsty, The Nab
- **Fell End** 2¼ miles/1350ft
  via Fell End Clouds, Sand Tarn
- **Aisgill Moor** 3 miles/1400ft
  *via Angerholme Pots,
  High Dolphinsty, The Nab*

- **Pendragon Castle** 3¾ miles/1650ft *via Little Fell, The Nab*
- **Hazelgill** 3 miles/1500ft *via High Dolphinsty, The Nab*

Swarth Fell
- **Grisedale** 2¾ miles/1100ft *via Flust, Swarth Fell Pike*

The Settle-Carlisle Railway permits an excellent linear walk over both fells, alighting at Garsdale and finishing at Kirkby Stephen

WALK 21 *7½ miles/1950ft from Garsdale Foot*

BAUGH FELL *2224ft/678m*

Start from Longstone Common, large parking area on A684
SD 694911; LA10 5NS ***Map: OL19***

While Baugh Fell may look extensive on the map, that is nothing compared to when underfoot. The fell is so independent it's almost moated: the River Clough rises in Grisedale to the east then flows the long miles of Garsdale along the fell's uniform southern base. The River Rawthey, meanwhile, flows west through Uldale then south through Rawtheydale. Water features range from East Tarns just beneath the summit to isolated West Baugh Fell Tarn, and down to mighty Uldale Force on the infant Rawthey. Its western flanks host parallel streams forming distinctive ravines, with Hebblethwaite Hall Gill notable. For many years the One-Inch map led to believe the summit was Knoutberry Haw with its OS column: however, the supposedly inferior Tarn Rigg Hill has proven to lift itself a couple of metres higher. The name is pronounced 'Bo', as in Lakeland's Bowfell – though there the similarity ends! *From Garsdale Foot*

BAUGH FELL • WALK 21

From the outset, Baugh Fell exerts a massive presence along Garsdale's northern slopes. Descend the side road dropping to cross the lively River Clough by Danny Bridge. It rises briefly steeply up the other side to an unsigned junction at Danny Brow. Double back left here, quickly swinging uphill to end at two driveways, with the house at Garsdale Foot to your right. A gate in front puts you onto open fell, where the onward 'road' (not used) resumes left as a grassy way. Your way is the grassy track rising away, with a stream and wall just to your right. It quickly swings right and runs on to cross the stream to a gate. Don't follow it across the stream, but rise left on a rougher quad track. This instantly falters, but a thinner trod continues rising gently with the fence to your right. Joined by the stream, you soon arrive at a rough quad track coming in from the left. Continue up to a fence corner, and remain with it as it swings right to commence a long, uncomplicated ascent towards your skyline objective. Though the track quickly fades, a clear little path rises ever gently with the fence to where a wall comes in to replace it. In time this will lead unfailingly to the summit.

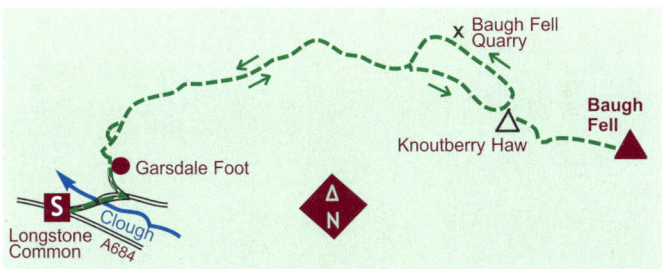

Just a few yards higher, the trod crosses Ringing Keld Gutter at the start of its little ravine. With an ascending quad track just yards to your left, this time it remains true, and will convey you all the way to that skyline. Never more than a stone's throw from the stream and wall, this endless steady rise features only modest moist moments. A distinct cairn sits on Garsdale Pike ahead right, while looking back, Middleton Fell offers a good appraisal of Combe Scar gouged from its flank. The principal feature however is the magnificent array of the Howgill Fells across Rawtheydale. Higher, the track is deflected left by a sidestream, but will later resume more directly up to approach the wall again.

At the foot of the steeper upper slopes the track performs an accommodating zigzag, then fades on easing out. A thin trod keeps faith with the wall on an even gentler rise. The broad west ridge is seen running north, backed by the curious flat top of Wild Boar Fell. At one

WALK 21 • BAUGH FELL

point the trod forks left from the wall to avoid a brief marshy section, then passing a rash of stones you quickly arrive at the stone-built Ordnance Survey column on Knoutberry Haw, Baugh Fell's west top at 2218ft/676m. Having a little more identity than the true summit, it offers views westwards to Sedbergh and its lovely environs where the rivers Rawthey and Clough meet, with the Howgill Fells inevitably dominant. While shapely Pen-y-ghent appears only on arrival here, Ingleborough is a notable absentee hidden behind Whernside.

The elusive summit on Tarn Rigg Hill is finally seen two-thirds of a mile to the east. The wall remains an infallible guide, largely shadowed by a quad track. After a grassy descent to a minor saddle featuring colourful pools, keep to the trod around an inner wall corner to then rise through minor peaty moments to gain the characterless summit. The high point is 20 yards past a tiny kink in the wall at a junction with a wall departing south. A single stone is usurped by a tiny cairn beneath the other side of the wall. A fine prospect of Dales mountains has Ingleborough now slotted in to see the Three Peaks tidily arranged, while Morecambe Bay features two sections split by Middleton Fell. On gently declining slopes to the north are the scattered East Tarns.

Uldale is a side valley gracing the opening miles of the River Rawthey as it curves around the base of Baugh Fell. Its beginnings carve a deep incision into the heart of the mountain, then going on to the limestone gorge of Dockholmes. A little further downstream is the magical plunge of Uldale Force.

BAUGH FELL • WALK 21

Uldale Force on the infant River Rawthey in Uldale

WALK 21 • BAUGH FELL

The return is largely as you came, other demanding options being either to remain on the wallside track east to descend into Grisedale, or drop north to the beginnings of Rawthey Gill to follow the infant River Rawthey through to Rawthey Bridge. On a nice day an interesting, pathless loop strikes north from the OS column on Knoutberry Haw, gently down for a quarter-mile to several cairns amid old workings, with a pool just below. Here strike west the short way to the site of Baugh Fell Quarry, which proves to be surprisingly extensive with massive piles of stones and old stone huts. Leave by resuming west for less than five minutes to find yourself on the modest but well defined scarp, with a handful of scattered rocks.

At East Tarns on Baugh Fell

Baugh Fell Quarry, looking west to the Howgill Fells

BAUGH FELL • WALK 21

Baugh Fell from Swarthgill in Garsdale

The wall is just two minutes to your left, or simply slant left down this grassy slope to pick up the quad track that will lead back. When you reach the end of the wall, don't be tempted to remain on the quad track, as it later encounters marshy terrain: instead re-cross the stream to follow the fenceside path back down. Also, after the bend near the bottom, you might remain on the rough quad track, as the fenceside path is in any case easily missed. This curves around and quickly drops to rejoin your outward route at the firmer track where it crosses the stream. This will quickly lead you back through the opening stage.

Alternative ascents
- **Rawthey Bridge**
  6 miles/1750ft
  *via Uldale Force,
  Rawthey Gill, East Tarns*
- **Grisedale**
  4 miles/1150ft
  *via High Flust,
  Haskhaw Gill*
- **Grisedale**
  2½ miles/1150ft
  via Grisedale Pike

WALK 22 *7 miles/2450ft from Cautley*

Yarlside
Randygill Top

2096ft/639m
2047ft/624m

Start from Cross Keys Inn on A683, lay-by just to north
SD 698969; LA10 5LY ***Map: OL19***

Yarlside and Randygill Top form the high eastern range of the Howgill Fells, linked by the shapely lesser top of Kensgriff. Ridges continue northwards to Hooksey and to Green Bell (1985ft/605m), source of the River Lune, with slopes falling towards the river's first villages of Ravenstonedale and Newbiggin-on-Lune. The extremely long valley of Bowderdale runs uniformly to the west. To the south, Yarlside brings the group to an abrupt and dramatic termination, with its enviable position overlooking the priceless Cautley scene. Whilst Cautley Crag and Spout belong to Calders, Yarlside wins hands-down as a vantage point. Both mountains have rounded tops, though Yarlside does show a rougher side to the east, overlooking the valley of Backside Beck. The name Yarlside may be Norse for Earl Seat, while Randygill Top is named from a stream that falls into the upper reaches of Bowderdale. ***From under The Calf***

YARLSIDE & RANDYGILL TOP • WALK 22

From the parking area, wooden steps drop to a footbridge over the River Rawthey. Pause already to appraise Great Dummacks downstream: a shoulder of Calders, this is the fell that boasts Cautley Crag as its own. Across, a good path heads away downstream above the river, quickly swinging in to the prized amphitheatre beneath Cautley Crag and Spout. Passing above a footbridge on Cautley Holme Beck, the path is drawn towards the base of the falls, surmounting a gentle spur that undulates along almost to the foot of the ravine. As it starts to climb through bracken, the path quickly forks. While the left branch crosses Bowderdale Gill to access the Spout, instead remain on the right branch continuing to climb through bracken. This gives a classic prospect of the tumbling falls of the Spout, with the upper pair of falls soon revealed. The path slants up above the sidestream as a delectable green way, zigzagging and becoming a little stony part way up to ease out on the featureless saddle of Bowderdale Head.

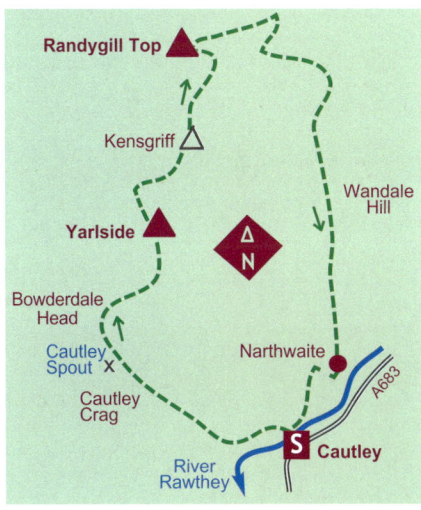

The now thin path advances along the near side of the saddle until just short of the highest point, where the second half of the ascent now begins. A thin but clear trod slants up to the right, crossing towards the largely grassy ravine between yourself and Yarlside's main bulk. Higher, it then contours almost to the upper ravine, and fades. Simply turn directly uphill on steeper grassy slopes to your right, soon easing out to advance to a small cairn and a pool on Yarlside's rounded south top. Just beyond, a thin path runs left to a minor saddle before a short, pleasant pull onto Yarlside's summit, marked by a lonely cairn. This otherwise bare top is a fine, airy vantage point, with Great Dummacks, Calders, Bram Rigg Top and The Calf behind, and the northern Howgills ridges arrayed. Eastwards are Howgills' neighbours Wild Boar, Swarth and Baugh Fells, while more distantly are the Lakeland Fells, Eden Valley and North Pennines featuring Cross Fell.

WALK 22 • YARLSIDE & RANDYGILL TOP

The approach path from Cautley, looking to Cautley Crag and Spout

Resume north-west on a thin path dropping very gently along the ridge, avoiding thoughts of a bee-line for Kensgriff, next along the ridge, due to the unseen roughness below. You are now amid a real Howgills atmosphere, with ridges and tops outspread, and looking directly down Bowderdale. Shapely Kensgriff is currently dwarfed by your present fell, but not so in ten minutes time when looking up at it! The path almost peters out on the abrupt northerly edge, so now slant right down steep grassy slopes to the col. A few marshy strides see a thin path make a pleasant ascent of 275ft to Kensgriff's small cairn at 1883ft/574m. Looking back, it will be seen why the direct approach was inadvisable, Yarlside's scree slope being too rough for comfort.

Resume north again, with a quad track descending the easy-angled ridge towards a saddle containing a couple of pools beneath Randygill Top's tame slopes. Remain on the main track to the left side of the broad ridge, aiming for the left edge of the saddle. Cross, briefly faintly, through a tiny peaty patch to the base of the steeper grassy slopes. The track now embarks on a straightforward direct ascent of some 400ft. Part way up, the quad track veers off left, but a continuing path maintains the short climb. This soon eases to reveal Randygill Top's summit just ahead, yet another lonely, solid cairn. The lowest of the five Howgills' mountains boasts a panorama as good as any, from the uninterrupted Lakeland skyline to the Westmorland Plateau, Eden Valley and North Pennines, and all around the northern Dales.

YARLSIDE & RANDYGILL TOP • WALK 22

Cautley Crag from the path at Bowderdale Head

Leave on the main, right-hand of two departing paths heading north-east past the tiny summit pool, and declining gently towards the prominent Green Bell. This grand high-level traverse on a sumptuous green path drops steadily to a well-defined narrow saddle under rounded Stockless. At this very point drop right a mere forty strides to pick up the beginnings of a trod marked as a public footpath on the map. Turn right on this to run a splendid course across Randygill Top's upper flanks, contouring along high above the beginnings of Stockless

Yarlside and its south top from above Cautley Crag

WALK 22 • YARLSIDE & RANDYGILL TOP

Looking across to The Calf from the ascent of Kensgriff

Gill. It then drops a little to the head of a grassy ravine, to then open out on easier slopes. With your earlier saddle just in front, leave the contouring path and slant left down the short way to cross a streamlet emerging from the base of a prominent reedy patch at the head of the gill. Across, a broad grassy way leads down above the gill. Soon fading, forge on down the slope, well above the beck and keeping right of reedy

Yarlside and Kensgriff from Mountain View

YARLSIDE & RANDYGILL TOP • WALK 22

Waterfall in Spen Gill

tracts. Aiming for Spen Gill ravine ahead, a confluence with Stockless Gill soon appears beneath it. The final stage drops more steeply to this fine spot, where waterfalls tumble through rocky surrounds.

Across the confluence a rough track slants right the short way to a fence enclosing new tree plantings, then trace the fence up to a corner. Now level, just yards to your right you join a grassy track on Wandale Hill's flank. Note that from the confluence crossing you could first go left up the bank to see more of the ravine and its waterfalls before crossing reedy ground to find the track. Turn right along it, the initial

WALK 22 • YARLSIDE & RANDYGILL TOP

Cautley Spout

Kensgriff and Yarlside from Randygill Top

stages being intermittently marshy until the fence drops away. A contrastingly splendid green march takes over, with Yarlside and Kensgriff well displayed to your right. The track largely maintains its contour with a parallel wall coming in below. Crossing minor sidestreams you merge with the wall to run high above the derelict farmhouse of Mountain View sat in its superlative location.

The way continues now just as a path, rising slightly as the wall drops away to reach a waymarked fork. Angle gently right down to a gate, with lovely Rawtheydale highly prominent ahead. The wall is traced down to a gate through which a sunken way drops the short way to the farm of Narthwaite. Entering

YARLSIDE & RANDYGILL TOP • WALK 22

The Cross Keys Inn at Cautley, beneath Yarlside

the yard, turn right between barns to a gate down to the right into a grassy enclosure. A grass track winds down to the bottom right corner, where an enclosed way drops to a ford on Backside Beck. Reasonable stepping-stones make for an easy crossing under normal conditions, though in spate expect wet feet (the alternative would be to take Narthwaite's drive to the road at Handley's Bridge). With the end just minutes away, the path doubles back left outside the trees and then contours delightfully on through open country. Now back on Yarlside's base, drop gently back to the opening steps by the Rawthey footbridge.

Alternative ascents

Yarlside
- **Cautley** 1½ miles/1550ft
  via Ben End

Randygill Top
- **Newbiggin-on-Lune**
  3¾ miles/1450ft
  via Pinskey, Green Bell
- **Weasdale** 3 miles/1350ft
  via Stwarth, Green Bell
- **Weasdale** 2½ miles/1400ft *via Hooksey, Leathgill Bridge*
- **Ravenstonedale** 4 miles/1350ft *via Thornthwaite, Stockless*

WALK 23

8½ miles/2550ft from Sedbergh

CALDERS
THE CALF

2211ft/674m
2218ft/676m

Start from the town centre, car parks
SD 658921; LA10 5AD   Map: OL19

The Calf marks the summit of the Howgill Fells, and fittingly claims a pivotal position in this enchanting group of hills. Its ascent from Sedbergh makes a splendid introduction to the area, though the hill remains hidden by neighbouring Calders almost to the end. Ridges and spurs radiate in all directions: the main spine crosses subsidiary Bram Rigg Top (2205ft/672m) en route to Calders, and a fine ridge runs north-west to connect with neighbouring Fell Head by way of subsidiary Bush Howe (2044ft/623m). Slopes fall north-east to the col of Bowderdale Head, where the group's second significant ridge begins on Yarlside. Running northwards is the long West Fell ridge dividing Bowderdale and Langdale, valleys much less frequented than the latter's Lakeland namesake! Calders' prized asset (well appraised at the start of Walk 22) is majestic Cautley Crag, featuring the superb falls of Cautley Spout. ***From Bluecaster***

CALDERS & THE CALF • WALK 23

Leave the main street by Joss Lane rising past the main car park. It swings right and along to leave suburbia at a gate, where an access road takes over. Here take the track slanting left to the top corner of the field. Ignoring its left turn, take a corner stile sending an enclosed path climbing away. It emerges to rise delightfully above the tree-lined Settlebeck Gill, at the top gaining the open fell at an iron kissing-gate under Winder's steep flank. With a choice of paths, take the grassy one slanting left. Rapidly reaching a fork, leave the ongoing green way in favour of an initially stonier one doubling back up to the right. This super path quickly eases to commence a sustained steady rise across the flank of Winder, parallel with the deep enclave of Settlebeck Gill.

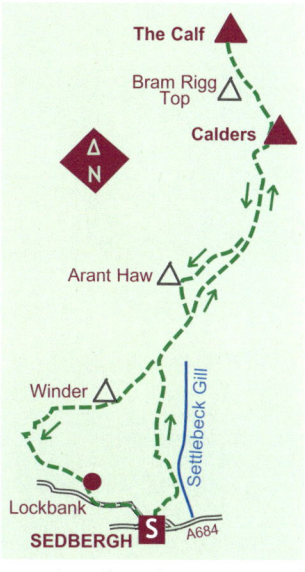

Crossing a streamlet the path runs closer to the edge of the ravine, into a more expansive upland. Just a little higher it swings to rise more directly and steeply, ignoring a branch left for Winder. It soon eases out at a junction on a col connecting Winder with Arant Haw ahead. Bear right to resume uphill to reach a major fork directly beneath Arant Haw. You shall return over this, so for now take the inviting right branch, which here commences a superb, prolonged slant across the slope to ultimately level out on Arant Haw's eastern shoulder. This reveals your objective of Calders across the dip of Rowantree Grains. The drop thereto is modest, featuring a stonier spell then across the dip to be joined by a fence. A steeper climb with it becomes stony nearer to the top, swinging right with the fence to emerge at Calders' summit cairn. This is a superbly sited vantage point on the edge of a pronounced drop, outdoing The Calf itself by virtue of its more detached setting, offering a more intimate picture of the valley scenery near Sedbergh.

Only now is your ultimate goal of the hitherto elusive Calf finally revealed some three-quarters of a mile further. While the fence turns off, your wide, stony path runs on, dipping to a very minor depression then rising onto the shoulder of Bram Rigg Top, whose summit is just to the left. Now dropping to another modest saddle from where paths

137

WALK 23 • CALDERS & THE CALF

radiate, yours goes straight on a very brief climb. Levelling out, it reveals the Ordnance Survey column just a minute further. The actual highest point is claimed to be a grassy patch some 20 yards to the south-east. Paths head off both north-west and north-east, with an often-dry pool just beyond. The view is wonderfully extensive, though gentle slopes in the immediate vicinity preclude anything dramatic. The panorama features the Cross Fell group to the north and the widely spread hills of the Dales to east and south, but on a clear day it is the serrated Lakeland skyline to the west that will claim attention beyond the Lune Valley: Morecambe Bay is well seen.

Named from a small hamlet just beneath their western flanks, the **Howgill Fells** occupy the north-western corner of the Yorkshire Dales. They stand apart in every sense from their typical Dales' neighbours, with the gritstone/limestone coalition replaced by slate beneath their rounded features. Triangular in shape, the group is moated by the River Lune on two sides and the Rawthey on the other. The terrain of this walkers' paradise is such that it encourages long strides over its grassy ridges, a lack of internal walls instilling a different sense of freedom to the rest of the Dales. Rarely in evidence is the underlying slate, though when revealed it is in spectacular style, at the quite remarkable ravines of Cautley (Walk 22) and Carlin Gill (Walk 24). Hub of this otherwise sparsely populated district is Sedbergh, largest community in the national park, which sits regally at the foot of its fells and presides over the convergence of several rivers.

CALDERS & THE CALF • WALK 23

The approach to Calders from the shoulder of Arant Haw

Leave by retracing steps first to Calders, and then back through Rowantree Grains up onto the shoulder of Arant Haw. Just short of the brow, leave the main path for a grassier but clear one bearing gently right up and along to Arant Haw's summit cairn at 1985ft/605m, less than half a mile further. This stage enjoys grand views to the right of

Looking west from Rowantree Grains Fold on the ascent to Calders

WALK 23 • CALDERS & THE CALF

Cautley Spout and Crag combine to form the grandest scene in the Howgill Fells. The steep crag extends for the best part of a mile to an abrupt terminus at the Spout, where a series of spritely falls tumble in rapid succession for several hundred feet to the floor of the valley. A well made path climbs steeply alongside them. Boasting one of the grandest settings in the Dales, and virtually in the shadow of the crag, the white-walled Cross Keys Inn is that very rare phenomenon the temperance inn, with a 1732 datestone and a warm welcome.

CALDERS & THE CALF • WALK 23

On the summit of The Calf

the western cirque of high Howgills, from Fell Head around to Calders. More distantly, the long Lakeland skyline features Black Combe, the Coniston Fells, the Scafells and Great Gable, with the Helvellyn group over Ill Bell and High Street.

Arant Haw from the Dales Way at Bramaskew in the Lune Valley

WALK 23 • CALDERS & THE CALF

Looking up to Winder from Sedbergh

Leave by turning sharp left, a few level strides seeing a path form as you look down on Winder, to drop quite steeply and directly to briefly rejoin your outward route. Drop right to the Winder col, and once again abandon your ascent route by remaining on the broad 'ridge' path making the short, very pleasant ascent over grassy knolls to Winder's summit. At 1551ft/473m it is crowned by an Ordnance Survey column and a Millennium topograph. The superb panorama includes a fine prospect up to the Lune Gorge and less frequented western Howgills. Garsdale and Dentdale are particularly appealing as they burrow deep into the higher fells of the Dales.

The Calf, Bram Rigg Top and Calders from Castley, to the west

CALDERS & THE CALF • WALK 23

Settlebeck Gill near the start of the walk

Leave by the onward grassy path striking west towards the Lune. This descends with increasing style and remarkable rapidity to the bracken zone and a little further to within a few yards of the intake wall. Turn left to find a slim path crossing a couple of small streams, then contouring on through bracken and a third streamlet above the wall. Sedbergh appears ahead, and as the bracken ends a quad track is joined, slanting down to meet the wall. It shadows it down to the bottom corner, where a gate accesses the rear of Lockbank Farm. A short enclosed way drops to a gate into the yard, then down the farm drive onto Howgill Lane, turning left to finish.

Alternative ascents

The Calf
- **Cautley** 2½ miles/1700ft via Cautley Spout, Force Gill Beck
- **Howgill** 3½ miles/2050ft via Birkhaw, Bram Rigg
- **Howgill** 3 miles/1950ft via Castley, White Fell
- **Bowderdale** 5½ miles/1650ft via Bowderdale Beck
- **Bowderdale** 5¼ miles/1800ft via West Fell, Hazelgill Knott

Calders
- **Cautley** 2¾ miles/1700ft via Cautley Spout, Cautley Crag
- **Howgill** 3½ miles/2000ft via Birkhaw, Bram Rigg
- **Howgill** 3½ miles/2000ft via Birkhaw, Arant Haw

WALK 24

5 miles/2050ft from Carlingill

FELL HEAD

2100ft/640m

Start from Carlingill Bridge, on Fairmile Road south of A685 at Low Borrowbridge. Parking areas on common to south
SD 624995; CA10 3XX *Map: OL19*

Western outlier of the Howgill Fells, Fell Head occupies an enviable setting on the edge of this delectable group. Attached to The Calf by an undulating high-level ridge, they could be linked in an ascent from the hamlet of Howgill: however, this hill is sufficiently independent to fully justify its own day, encouraged by the superb ravines secreted in the folds of Carlin Gill under the northern flanks. Fell Head overlooks the Lune Gorge with its contrasting modes of travel. Fairmile Road along the base of the fell traces a Roman road, while immediately beyond the lovely river are the West Coast Main Line and the more intrusive M6 motorway. Fell Head's slopes are frequented by the further contrasts of free-roaming fell ponies and the aerial antics of paragliders.

From Crook of Lune Bridge

FELL HEAD • WALK 24

Note that this is not a walk for the genteel, and the Carlin Gill ravine could be dangerous in wet or wintry conditions: an escape option is mentioned at the end of the first paragraph.

From the single-arched bridge follow the south bank of Carlingill Beck upstream, with a rough little path materialising. An early impasse forces you higher through bracken, meeting a better path that slants left back down to the bank. Ignoring its final grassy drop to the colourful confluence with Weasel Gill, contour around through bracken to slant gently down to the beck. Resuming, though progress is slow this lengthy approach to the ravines is largely a delight between tight but not claustrophobic slopes. An intermittent path encounters a few rocks to clamber over, with the route never in question. As slopes ease, the thin path makes easier progress at a slightly higher level after crossing the minor sidestream of Haskaw Gill. It runs on to a notable confluence with Small Gill, a lovely spot marked by a cairn and meriting a break before events turn more dramatic. An escape option would be to trace the side gill uphill, or the grassy spur in between the two streams.

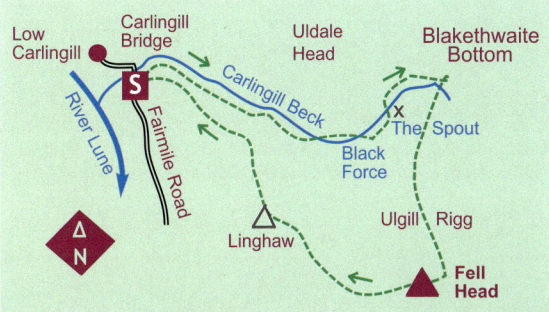

Advance just a very short way further to an obvious crossing point onto the opposite bank of the now deeply carved gill. A clear little path rises above a rocky impasse and on through a small patch of scree. This cautious but delectable traverse quickly leads to the foot of the ravine of Black Force on the opposite bank. Keeping faith with the floor of Carlin Gill, a small path remains on the north side for a while, then at another rocky impasse it crosses to forge spiritedly on through the bouldery environs of the narrow floor. The gill soon bends right to pass a lovely waterslide, and this absorbing path is soon halted at the emphatic impasse of The Spout, depositing you neatly at a perfectly placed natural viewing platform. This stunning waterfall is not fully seen until penetrating to this limit of exploration.

WALK 24 • FELL HEAD

Escape by crossing the stream below the viewing platform to a choice of a steep, grassy pull or a scramble up a groove in a tilted slab. Either demands caution, while the latter earns a more intimate view of The Spout. Rise left of a higher, smaller slab onto easier ground, then slant right above that slab into gentle surrounds above the waterfall. Whilst you might simply turn right through the upper stream's easing ravine, you could also ascend steep grass alongside a heathery spread to meet a sheeptrod, turning right to contour along to the reedy hollow of Blakethwaite Bottom. After the claustrophobia of Carlin Gill, this is a contrastingly spacious upland. Without entering on the continuing trod, drop right across the lesser, left-hand beck above the confluence. A thin trod curves around a minor knoll above the main arm, Great Ulgill Beck, to meet a path bearing right to an obvious crossing point.

Rise briefly away on the slender path to a small reedy patch. Ignore a little path heading off right, and instead make a short, steep pull up the bank to the left. This rapidly eases as a clear trod slants slightly right up the spur. Fell Head is up to the left, and Carlin Gill's depths hidden down to the right. The way soon briefly levels out in front of another reedy patch: here opt for an initially thinner but clear trod slanting left up onto Ulgill Rigg. This climbs away, crossing a more direct uphill quad track, then fading on reaching a broad, tilted shelf. Simply continue up, bearing left to pick up the quad track which can be seen rising all the way ahead. Soon steepening, ignore any lesser branches as the track makes a sustained ascent of the easy slopes. Looking back, the most tranquil of Howgills scenes features a group of almost identical, unfrequented lesser tops.

Fell Head from The Calf

FELL HEAD • WALK 24

Carlin Gill remains a relatively unknown feature secreted in the folds of the Howgill Fells. Whilst the entire gill is a colourful location with heathery patches, it boasts two remarkable, aptly named physical features. The Spout pours into a rugged amphitheatre that is one of the finest places to be in the whole Yorkshire Dales, while Black Force is a contrasting series of tumbling little falls throughout the length of a substantial sidestream in a dark-walled gorge.

WALK 24 • FELL HEAD

Only at the very top does the track fade, literally within yards of a sudden arrival on the well-defined summit ridge, with a big open view of The Calf group ahead. The summit cairn stands just 250 yards to the right along a broad ridge path. A particular attraction of Fell Head is that despite its natural high-level link to the main massif, it has a very independent, detached feel to it. Its 'outpost' situation makes it a superb all-round viewpoint, not only for its Howgills' neighbours, but also looking down on the Lune Gorge, across to the unfrequented Whinfell Ridge and little known Borrowdale, all backed by the distant Lakeland skyline.

Fell pony and paraglider, Fell Head
Right: Black Force in Carlin Gill

FELL HEAD • WALK 24

Carlingill Beck and Uldale Head from Carlingill Bridge

Depart by continuing along the ridge, through a minor dip and quickly up to a lesser cairn on the western top. Descent proper begins directly from it on an initially thin trod dropping north-west, bound for the distinct knoll of Linghaw some distance below. This delectable path winds invitingly down Fell Head's north-western spur of Blake Ridge, quickly becoming a clearer quad track. Ignoring a lesser fork right, it drops unfailingly to a saddle in front of Linghaw. Keep straight on the quad track for the short pull of little over 100ft to its unmarked grassy brow at 1640ft/500m. Remain on the broad track maintaining the same downhill direction, with the Lune Gorge outspread below. The finish is an obvious one, this infallible track tracing the long spine of the fell high above the Carlin Gill edge. For a while there is a good prospect up the ravine to The Spout. Only on the very lower slopes does the track falter: a trod maintains the line, broadening again and swinging a little left to run along to the road above the bridge.

Alternative ascents
- **Carlingill Bridge**
  2¹⁄4 miles/1650ft
  via Linghaw
- **Fairmile Gate**
  2 miles/1700ft
  via Fairmile Gill,
  Whin's End

WALK 25 *24¹⁄₂ miles/5300ft from Horton-in-Ribblesdale*

THE THREE PEAKS WALK
PEN-Y-GHENT, WHERNSIDE & INGLEBOROUGH

Start from the village centre, car park
SD 808726; BD24 0HF   Map: OL2

THREE PEAKS WALK • WALK 25

The Three Peaks are an iconic trio of mountains around Upper Ribblesdale, and the traditional objective is to complete their circuit within 12 hours. The challenge was set in 1887 by two Giggleswick schoolmasters whose epic stroll unwittingly created a Yorkshire classic. The well waymarked route has seen several changes in order to keep to rights of way and avoid eroded sections. Horton's Pen-y-ghent Café has long been the favoured start point, its owners and clocking-in machine being the stuff of legend. Though currently closed, hopefully it will return at some point. Horton remains the obvious starting point, with Ribblehead being the most practical alternative.

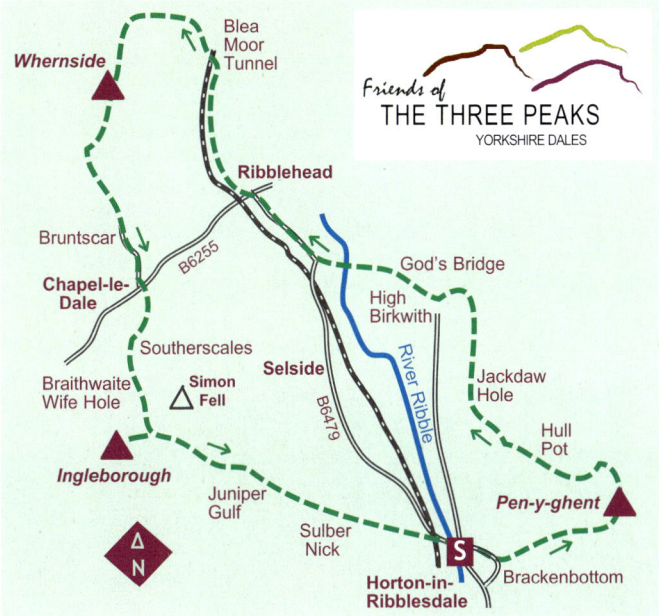

Summer weekends can see the circuit overrun with sponsored and commercial large-scale group events, resulting in massive overcrowding with its attendant problems. Whilst the paths also suffer, these days much of the route is almost bombproof thanks to the National Park's Three Peaks Project. Decades of toil have stabilised many miles of paths, and their sterling efforts can be acknowledged with a donation towards ongoing work at www.yorkshiredales.org.uk/threepeaks.

WALK 25 • THREE PEAKS WALK

Stage 1: Horton to Pen-y-ghent (2½ miles; 1525ft of ascent)

From the car park head south along the street past the Pen-y-ghent Café, and just after the campsite (but before the church), a small gate on the left sends a fieldside path to a small gate where the path drops down steps between houses onto a back lane. Go briefly left and cross a footbridge on Douk Gill, then go left on a parallel lane. This passes the former school and winds around above the beck to the hamlet of Brackenbottom. Before the first building take a gate on the left, with a bridle-gate up above it. This sends a built path steeply up a fieldside, remaining with the wall for the entire first half of the climb. Nearing a bridle-gate the gradient eases and the hill's magnificent profile returns. Two further bridle-gates in cross-walls are met, the path being largely stone-flagged or on firm chippings. Modest bands of limestone and a couple of level sections feature, and the climb's major turning point comes as you rise to a bridle-gate at the foot of the south ridge.

The gate sends a broad path left up the wallside for the big push, firstly alongside and up the edge of a limestone band featuring natural steps. This quickly puts you onto a shelf beneath a sprawling gritstone boulderfield. Again the path runs to the right side, then clambers up between them to engage hands to scale the gritstone band. Beyond this you are virtually on the top, and a simple stroll on a stone-flagged path leads up to the Ordnance Survey column and modern shelter.

Ascending Pen-y-ghent   Opposite: Leaving Pen-y-ghent for Ribblehead

THREE PEAKS WALK • WALK 25

Stage 2: Pen-y-ghent to Ribblehead (7¾ miles; 550ft of ascent)

Leave by crossing the stile and heading along the broad path slanting away. This quickly features a stone-flagged section down to a well-defined edge above gritstone outcrops, then deflects northwards to slant down to the limestone band. At a sharp bend left, look to the right for a glimpse of the spectacular finger of rock known as Pen-y-ghent Pinnacle. Your path now works straight down the fell, with the gaping hole of Hull Pot on the moor below. The path descends to a gate, then along the short way further to a gate just short of a path crossroads at the head of Horton Scar Lane. A few minutes to your right is the mighty chasm of Hull Pot, but ignore both that and the lane to resume up a surfaced path ahead. This bears away from the wall to a collapsed wall, with a wall corner to the right on Whitber Hill. The path drops to a wall junction, through which it bridges Sell Gill Beck and rises gently to contour around to the left. Dropping to a kissing-gate, it then drops steeply to a streamlet, and after a slight rise drops again onto the broad, partly grassy track of Harber Scar Lane.

Turn right on its broad, near-level course with a wall to your left, soon passing Jackdaw Hole across it. At a gate it becomes firmer, and a little further leave at a kissing-gate on the left. A clear path rises by a wall, this short section being a permissive path that is closed one day a year on 1st May. It drops to a corner stile, then across a large sheep pasture, passing above limestone scars to join a firm track. Bear left above Birkwith Cave's wooded environs to a corner gate/stile, and the track heads away with a wall to a junction. Go left a short way down to another junction above High Birkwith, then right with a wall above a wooded ravine. Resume through a gate at the end, but when the track quickly swings up to the right, take the clear path ahead. This drops gently by a wall to a gate at God's Bridge at the end, where Brow Gill Beck's little ravine ends as it sinks below a natural limestone bridge.

WALK 25 • THREE PEAKS WALK

A clear, broadening track continues away to wind down and along to approach Nether Lodge. The fading track sends a path right across Ling Gill Beck on an arched footbridge to a bridle-gate behind. The firm path then curves left outside the grounds to join the access road. Go right on this to bridge the River Ribble. A little further it swings left to a gate, then loops around a limestone knoll to double back right to Ingman Lodge (1667), continuing on its drive climbing the short way onto the B6479. Turn right for a long mile to Ribblehead, helped by some useful verge sections. The road drops down and around to the busy junction backed by Ribblehead Viaduct beneath Whernside's vast bulk. This is a major post, with a refreshment and/or ice-cream van (possibly), and the Station Inn (definitely) just to the left.

Setting out for Whernside alongside Ribblehead Viaduct

Stage 3: Ribblehead to Whernside (4¼ miles; 1550ft of ascent)

From the junction a path crosses to meet the broad track heading for the viaduct from the pub. Just before its arches, branch right on a clear path which makes a brief pull to then shadow the railway. It runs by the signal box at Bleamoor Sidings before straying a little from the line, running to a footbridge on Little Dale Beck before tracing Force Gill the short way to an aqueduct just short of Blea Moor Tunnel. Across the aqueduct the reconstructed path rises to a gate in a fence above the tunnel entrance, with a good view of Force Gill's splendid waterfall. The path runs left to commence the ascent proper, with a fence replacing the wall on your left. The summit ridge returns to view, and at a stile in the fence, cross to resume on the main path.

THREE PEAKS WALK • WALK 25

The restored path climbs more steadily to meet a fence and old wall, just before landing on a broad shelf. The path then slants left with the fence/wall to cross a streamlet before the onset of a long series of stone flags cut another corner of the fence/wall. The sizeable Greensett Tarn soon appears to your left in Whernside's lap. The flags climb to rejoin the fence/wall on the northern extremity of Whernside's mighty summit ridge, and the finest section sees the path traverse the crest of the increasingly steep eastern plunge. Only a little more effort is needed to gain the summit by increasingly easy and enjoyable walking. The now intact wall shadows the final stage along to a shelter, with the Ordnance Survey column found through a stile in a kink of the wall.

Leaving Whernside's summit bound for Ingleborough

Stage 4: Whernside to Chapel-le-Dale (2¾ miles; 75ft of ascent)

Resume on the broad and stony wallside path dropping steadily away, quickly passing through a kissing-gate as the wall makes a brief dog-leg before returning. Continue for some time before two short, stone-pitched drops. At the foot of the second, the path bears left off the ridge to commence a rapid descent to the valley. The initially steep, pitched path drops to a bridle-gate in a wall, below which a better graded, often stone-flagged way affords easier progress. This longer section drops to another gate, below which a final pasture is crossed to a far corner gate beyond limestone outcrops. Go briefly right to a T-junction of ways alongside a limekiln just short of Bruntscar. Turn left down the access road past large barns, and becoming surfaced at a cattle-grid at the bottom, it runs gently out through the fields. With Ingleborough beckoning ahead, it passes Philpin Farm with its vending refreshment shed to join the B6255 at Chapel-le-Dale.

WALK 25 • THREE PEAKS WALK

Stage 5: Chapel-le-Dale to Ingleborough (2½ miles; 1450ft of ascent)

Turn briefly left to the Hill Inn, and just 30 yards further a wall-stile on the right sends a grassy path away, rising above a wall to meet a grassy bridleway at a gate. Ingleborough's majestic stance either fires or deflates the spirits, depending on your condition. Through the gate a gentle green way runs on through two further gates between lush limestone pastures to enter Southerscales Nature Reserve. Further, a firmer track rises gently beneath a limestone scar, swinging left then right across the edge of the Southerscales pavement. It runs on past the massive shakehole of Braithwaite Wife Hole to a bridle-gate onto the fell, and a sudden transition from limestone pasture to austere fellside.

A stone-flagged path takes up the running, soon interrupted by a level boardwalk across an exceedingly moist tract. The flags return to remain a constant during alternating steeper and gentler sections, to end abruptly at a wall corner at Humphrey Bottom. A stone-pitched path takes over to scale exceptionally steep slopes close by a streamlet, emerging with relief on the dramatic edge of the broad ridge running north to Simon Fell. The stream is crossed to a kissing-gate where wall and fence meet, and the final stage awaits. Still largely stone surfaced, the path climbs right up the slope of Swine Tail. As it steepens, just short of tumbled boulders above, is a modest standing stone: this is the junction of the Horton path to which you will return from the summit. Bearing right beneath the boulders, you emerge onto Ingleborough's tilted summit plateau. A path rises along the right edge past a massive cairn, with another large one at a substantial section of ancient wall: the summit shelter is now in sight, and is equally rapidly gained.

Approaching Ingleborough's summit plateau

Stage 6: Ingleborough to Horton (4¾ miles; 100ft of ascent)

Retrace steps across the plateau and down to the standing stone, where bear right on the varyingly surfaced path dropping away. It soon eases out for a sustained, near-level traverse of Simon Fell Breast. From a wall-stile at the end the path drops steadily away, joined by a wall to drop to a ruinous shooting box at Juniper Gulf. A little beyond that, you ford the adjacent stream to a gate. 150 yards further, keep left at a fork as the main path commences a brief, virtually level peaty section. It is then briefly squeezed by limestone alongside the adjacent wall to a bridle-gate into Ingleborough National Nature Reserve. Still largely level, the improving path heads away by modest limestone pavements, and along to drop to Sulber path crossroads: only two miles remain.

Advance straight on the restored path through the trough of Sulber Nick, reaching a large cairn to drop to a bridle-gate in a wall. A little further, a prominent cairn on a knoll reveals part of the village, and the path drops to another cross-paths – into the final mile! Dropping to a gateway in a wall, you enter an extensive limestone landscape. With the aid of marker posts the path swings sharply right for some time, then curves left at a fork down to an outer wall corner. Turning sharp right, it slants down to a bridle-gate out of the reserve and into a field. The path undulates along to a bridle-gate in a wall, then crosses Beecroft Hall access road and across a lengthy pasture to another bridle-gate. Head away to drop briefly to a small gate down onto the railway, crossing with care to its access road down into the village. Follow the footway ahead to cross a footbridge on the Ribble by-passing two road bridges.

Congratulations!!

Into the final yards: Horton station with Pen-y-ghent beyond

OUT ON THE FELLS............

Buckden Pike

Pen-y-ghent

Swarth Fell